CONFLICT IN IRELAND

THIRD EDITION

FROM ORIGINS TO THE PEACE AGREEMENT

Tony McAleavy

Collins
Educational
An Imprint of HarperCollins*Publishers*

CONTENTS

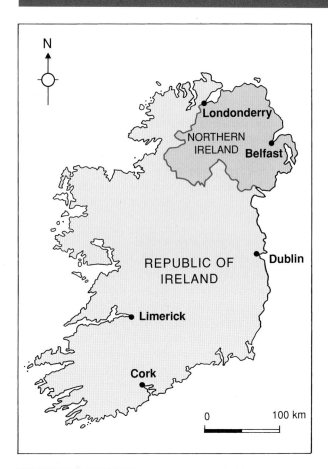

Northern Ireland is a small place, no larger than Yorkshire and with a population of about 1.5 million: less than that of a city like Birmingham or Glasgow. Yet despite its small size, since 1968 Northern Ireland has been a centre of the world's attention. TV and newspaper reporters from many countries have flocked there. The reason for all this media interest has been a violent conflict between the people of the province. This violence has been extremely intense. In the years 1968–94 over 3,000 people in Northern Ireland were killed in political violence and many more were injured. Why has the recent history of Northern Ireland been marred by so much bloodshed?

To make sense of the conflict in Ireland it is necessary to look at the way the different parts of Ireland are governed. The island of Ireland is divided between two different states:

The North
Northern Ireland is part of the United Kingdom. It is ruled by the British Parliament in London.

The South
The Republic of Ireland is an independent country, with its own government and parliament in Dublin.

Canary Wharf, London, February 1996: an IRA bomb causes massive damage and kills two people.
Why have arguments over Northern Ireland caused violence of this type?

What is it all about?

The recent violence in Ireland is all about one simple question:

SHOULD THE NORTH STAY PART OF THE UNITED KINGDOM OR SHOULD IT JOIN THE SOUTH AS PART OF A UNITED AND INDEPENDENT IRELAND?

This question has resulted in conflict for a number of reasons:

1. The people of Northern Ireland disagree about the future of Ireland. One side wants to stay part of the UK. They are called Unionists. Hardline Unionists are also known as Loyalists. Most of the Unionists are members of the Protestant community.

The other side want Northern Ireland to join the South and become part of the Irish Republic. They are called Nationalists. Hardline Nationalists are also known as Republicans. They are mostly members of the Catholic community.

2. The two groups in Northern Ireland are suspicious of each other. Some are very determined to get their own way. Although most people in Northern Ireland do not support violence, a minority of Loyalists and Republicans have used murder to show how strongly they feel about the future of Ireland.

3. The governments of the UK and the Irish Republic have often disagreed about Northern Ireland. The government in Dublin has always wanted a united Ireland. The British government has often said that it will not withdraw from Northern Ireland as long as a majority of the people of Northern Ireland wish to stay British.

4. Both Nationalists and Unionists say that they are 'democrats'. This means that they believe a majority should decide when there is an argument about politics. However, they disagree about who should be allowed a say. Nationalists think that a majority of all people in the whole of Ireland should be allowed to decide. Unionists believe that only people in Northern Ireland have a right to determine the future of Northern Ireland.

The two communities in Northern Ireland are represented by a large number of different organisations. These are often in the news. The fact that there are so many different organisations shows that people in Northern Ireland have a wide range of political opinions. Here is a list of the main organisations for the Nationalist and Unionist communities:

NATIONALIST/CATHOLIC

SDLP – Social Democratic and Labour Party:
Founded in 1970, the SDLP is supported almost entirely by Catholics. It wants Irish unity but is fiercely opposed to the violence of the IRA. It has influence with the government in Dublin and the US government. The SDLP is the main voice of peaceful Nationalism in Northern Ireland.

Sinn Féin:
This political party backs the tradition of revolutionary violence and the work of the IRA. It is supported by Catholics in working-class areas of Belfast and Derry and in some rural areas. Sinn Féin puts up candidates for elections throughout Ireland but it only receives significant support in some parts of the North.

IRA – Irish Republican Army:
Originally established in 1919, this organisation has used force to oppose the British presence in Ireland. IRA members have killed large numbers of British soldiers and Northern Ireland police officers. IRA bombs have also killed civilians in both Northern Ireland and mainland Britain. The IRA is illegal in both the UK and the Republic of Ireland.

UNIONIST/PROTESTANT

UUP – Ulster Unionist Party:
The Ulster Unionist Party was established in the late 19th century to defend the interests of northern Protestants. It is sometimes called the Official Unionist Party. The UUP ruled Northern Ireland between 1920 and 1971.

DUP – The Democratic Unionist Party:
The second most powerful Unionist party was founded in 1971 by Ian Paisley, and relied for much of its appeal on his powerful personality. The DUP has taken much working-class support away from the Ulster Unionist Party. It has taken a tough and uncompromising view and has called for the destruction of the IRA.

The Orange Order:
In 1795 the Orange Order was established to help protect Protestants. Today it is the largest Protestant organisation in Northern Ireland. It is named after the 17th-century Protestant king, William of Orange. It organises regular marches to celebrate the traditions of the Protestant community.

UDA/UVF – The Ulster Defence Association and the Ulster Volunteer Force:
These two groups are the main loyalist paramilitary groups. They were established in the early 1970s to fight the IRA. They are both illegal. Both groups have been responsible for the murder of innocent Catholics, in reprisal for the work of the IRA.

Nationalist/Catholic crowd on the streets of Northern Ireland. Why are they waving the Irish Republic's flag?

Unionist/Protestant supporters on a march. Which flag are they parading?

❖ *Explain in your own words how people in Northern Ireland disagree about how they should be governed.*

❖ *Look at the list of organisations on page 4. Can you find any examples of recent news stories involving some of these organisations. How can you tell from the stories that people in Northern Ireland are divided about their future?*

Key personalities in Northern Ireland

Gerry Adams: the President of Sinn Féin. As a young man he was involved in the IRA. Since then he has encouraged the Republican movement to become involved in constitutional politics.

John Hume: the leader of the SDLP. John Hume has been for many years the spokesman for the non-violent tradition of Irish nationalism.

David Trimble: the leader of the Ulster Unionist Party. His party is the largest Northern Ireland Party and has a number of MPs at Westminster.

Ian Paisley: the founder of the Democratic Unionist Party. Paisley has a very forceful personality and has played a central part in Northern Ireland politics since the 1960s.

Gerry Adams

Ian Paisley

Other players in the Irish conflict

The Alliance Party:
This small political party seeks support from both Catholics and Protestants. The Alliance Party is not in favour of a united Ireland but wants the two communities to share power in Northern Ireland.

RUC – Royal Ulster Constabulary:
The RUC is the Northern Ireland police force. Unlike the police in mainland Britain, RUC officers are often armed. The great majority of RUC members are Protestants. Many members of the RUC have been killed by the IRA. Some Nationalists distrust the RUC and would like to see the organisation replaced.

The Royal Irish Regiment:
This army regiment is recruited in Northern Ireland. Many of its members are part-timers. It has few Catholic members. It was set up in 1992 after the abolition of the part-time Ulster Defence Regiment (UDR). Many members of the UDR had been killed by the IRA.

The British Army:
Regular troops of the British Army were sent to Northern Ireland as a peace-keeping force in 1969. They soon became involved in the conflict and were often attacked by the IRA. After 1977 the army reduced its role and gave greater control over security to the RUC.

The British Secretary of State:
After 1972 the British government ruled directly over Northern Ireland. The effective ruler of the province became the British Cabinet Minister responsible for Northern Ireland. A series of politicians have held this post.

The view from Dublin and London

In the Republic of Ireland there are two large political parties – Fianna Fáil and Fine Gael. Both are Nationalist parties and both sympathise with the position of the Catholics in Northern Ireland. Traditionally Fianna Fáil has taken a tougher line on the need for Irish unification than Fine Gael. The third party in the Republic is the Irish Labour Party. The Labour Party has often formed a coalition government with one of the larger parties.

On the mainland of Britain there are three main political parties – the Conservatives, Labour and the Liberal Democrats. In recent times all three parties have tried not to disagree too much about Ireland. However, traditionally the Liberals and the Labour Party have been sympathetic to the idea of Irish Nationalism, while the Conservatives have been closer to the Unionists than the other two parties. In Wales and Scotland there are nationalists who would like to break away from the control of London, in a way similar to nationalists in Ireland. Welsh Nationalists support Plaid Cymru and Scottish Nationalists vote for the Scottish Nationalist Party. In contrast with Irish nationalism, Scottish and Welsh nationalism is almost exclusively peaceful.

The Dublin and London governments have long taken different views of the future of Northern Ireland:

SOURCE 1

In no event will Northern Ireland, or any part of it, cease to be part of the UK without the consent of the majority of the people in Northern Ireland voting in a poll.

The British government view, 1973

SOURCE 2

The Irish government does not and never will accept Britain's right to control any part of Irish territory. The right of the Irish nation to control the whole of Ireland has been stated over centuries and it will never be given up.

The Irish government view, 1969

❖ *What similarities and differences are there between Irish nationalism and Welsh or Scottish nationalism?*
❖ *What can we learn from Sources 1 and 2 about the different views of the British and Irish governments?*

SOURCE 3

Following the Good Friday Agreement it was intended to transfer power from the Secretary of State and the government in London to the Northern Ireland Assembly. Seamus Mallon, Northern Ireland's Deputy First Minister and David Trimble, First Minister with Mo Mowlam, Secretary of State for Northern Ireland and Tony Blair, Prime Minister.

A SHORT HISTORY OF THE IRISH CONFLICT

Stage 1 Invaders and settlers 100BC–1500 AD

Between 100BC–1500 AD three groups of settlers came to Ireland: Gaels, Vikings and Norman-English knights.

▶

Although this led to conflict, over time these groups intermarried and merged.

▶

By 1500 almost all Irish people followed a Gaelic way of life and the Catholic faith. The English government had little power over Ireland.

Stage 2 English conquest and colonisation 1500–1790

In the 16th century English Protestant rulers decided to take control of Ireland.

▶

They took land from the Catholic Irish and gave it to Protestant settlers from England and Scotland.

▶

By 1690 these Protestant settlers controlled the land and government of Ireland for the English kings.

Stage 3 The fight for Irish Independence

After 1790, two groups of Irish people began a struggle to free Ireland from British rule. They were called the NATIONALISTS.

1790–1914 Revolutionary Nationalists tried to win complete independence by rebellions. These all failed.

1820–1914 Parliamentary Nationalists tried to win a separate Irish parliament by peaceful persuasion.

▶

1790–1914 Irish Protestants, especially in the North, decided to fight to keep Ireland and Britain united. They were called UNIONISTS.

By 1914 it seemed that the Parliamentary Nationalists had forced the British Government to give Ireland a separate parliament. The First World War stopped this happening.

▶

After the war, in the 1918 election, the Revolutionary Nationalists won a surprise victory. They set up their own government in Dublin.

During a fierce guerrilla war 1919–21, British rule collapsed in much of Ireland – but not in Ulster. Here Unionists continued to oppose a break with Britain.

Stage 4 Ireland divided

North and South 1920–68

Since 1920–21 Ireland has been divided into two parts, North and South. The South became an independent country with a largely Catholic government.

▶

The North stayed linked to Britain. Protestant Unionists controlled the Northern Ireland government.

▶

Catholic Nationalists in the North were treated unfairly by the Protestant Unionists.

The troubles in the North since 1968

In 1968 trouble broke out in the North between Protestant Unionists and Catholic Nationalists.

▶

In 1969 the British government sent in troops to keep order. In 1972 they took power from the Protestants and began direct rule from Britain.

▶

In the decades that followed the IRA killed hundreds of soldiers, police and civilians. At the same time Protestant Unionist gangs killed many Catholic people.

9

WAVES OF SETTLEMENT 100 BC – AD1500

The people who live in Ireland today are descended from many different groups of settlers who crossed over to Ireland from Britain or the continent of Europe. Many members of the modern Catholic community see themselves as descendants of Gaelic or Celtic settlers.

The coming of the Gaels

The Celts (or Gaels) came to Ireland sometime during the centuries before the birth of Christ. They imposed their language on the existing Irish people and probably intermarried with them. Only a limited amount is known about these early Celts because they were illiterate and kept no written records of their deeds. Celtic stories, written down in later centuries, indicate that the Celts were divided into different kingdoms and tribal groups. The kingdoms were dominated by aristocratic warriors, who often did battle with each other. In the most famous of the early stories, the men of Ulster successfully defeat the men of Connacht.

The Gaelic invasion made a lasting impression on Ireland. A version of the language spoken by the Gaels is still used for everyday speech in parts of western Ireland. The language is now called 'Irish' and it is taught in most Catholic schools.

SOURCE 1

The mid-7th century Book of Durrow – a product of the Gaelic Golden Age.

SOURCE 2

Finn MacCool and his Fenians were a band of brave warriors in ancient Celtic legends, Like King Arthur's knights, they were sworn to fight for justice. In the 19th century, a group of Irish Nationalists who wanted to throw the British out of Ireland by force called themselves 'Fenians'. Why do you think they did this?

In the 5th century the Gaels became Christians and Christianity has been a powerful influence on Irish life ever since. According to ancient tradition, Christianity was brought by St Patrick. In fact this most 'Irish' of historical figures was another immigrant – probably from the west coast of Britain.

Between AD500 and 800 Gaelic Ireland became one of the most important centres of learning in Europe. Irish scholars and missionaries travelled across Europe setting up schools and monasteries.

Today Irish Nationalists are very proud of their Gaelic past and they feel it clearly sets them apart from the British. They look back on this 'golden age' as proof of what Irish people could do if only they were free from foreign interference.

SOURCE 3

I believe that it is our Gaelic past which is at the bottom of our heart. We must never forget that the Ireland of today is the descendant of 7th-century Ireland. The failure of Irish people in recent times is due to our ceasing to be Irish without becoming English.

Douglas Hyde, founder of the Gaelic League, 1894

The Viking and Norman invasions

This 'golden age' came to an end as a result of another invasion. From around 800, groups of Vikings began to arrive in Ireland. They were followed in 1167 by Norman knights, who crossed over to Ireland about 100 years after the Norman conquest of England. Vikings and Normans threatened the way of life of Ireland's Gaelic chiefs and their people. The Vikings were pagans. They repeatedly attacked the Christian monasteries of Ireland. The Normans owed loyalty to a king across the sea in England. In 1171 their king, Henry II of England, visited them and decided to call himself 'Lord of Ireland'.

In time both groups intermarried with the Gaelic Irish. The Vikings became Christians and set themselves up as traders in towns along the coast, including the town of Dublin. The Normans eventually learned to live like Gaelic chiefs. The kings of England hardly ever visited the country and, by the late Middle Ages, had little influence except in a small area around Dublin, known as 'the Pale'.

SOURCE 4

A Norman knight in Ireland – one in a long line of invaders.

SOURCE 5

While at the time of the conquest the invaders spoke their own language, now many of them have abandoned this and their way of life. Instead they use the customs and language of the Irish. They have married and allied themselves with the King's Irish enemies.

Adapted from the 'Laws of Kilkenny' which tried to stop Norman settlers mixing with native Irish people, 1336.

Ireland at the end of the Middle Ages

By 1500 the power of the English kings over Irish life 'beyond the Pale' had dwindled to virtually nothing. Ireland remained divided into a series of small kingdoms (some of them now ruled by Norman Irish families). The kingdoms of Ireland often fought against each other but their people shared a common language, culture and religion.

SOURCE 6

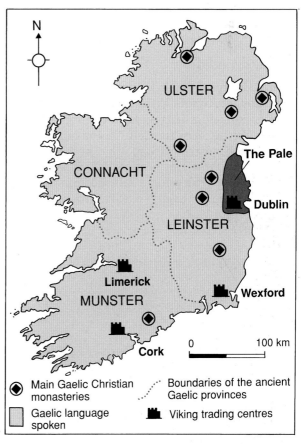

Ireland in 1500

* ❖ *Explain in your own words who the Celts were?*
* ❖ *Why do many modern Irish Catholics look back with pride to the history of Celtic Ireland?*
* ❖ *How did the government of England become involved in Irish politics? How far was England in control of Ireland at the end of the Middle Ages?*

REBELLIONS AND PLANTATIONS:
1500 – 1690

In the 16th century there was an important change in the relationship between the English and the Irish. English rulers began to take a closer interest in Ireland. The Tudor family had established firm control of England and Wales and wished to extend its power to the neighbouring island. Religious changes added a new element to the conflict. During the Reformation of the 16th century, Europe became divided into Catholic and Protestant countries. England cut all links with the Roman Catholic Church and became a Protestant country. Most of Ireland, however, remained staunchly Catholic and there was a real danger that Ireland would be used as a base to attack England by her Catholic enemies in Europe, particularly Spain. English worries were summed up by a proverb of the time:

> *He who would England win*
> *Must with Ireland begin.*

Tudor expeditions

Henry VIII made the first move in a long campaign to control the Irish. In 1541 he changed his title from 'Lord' to 'King of Ireland' and told the Irish chieftains that they must all obey his orders. His children, Edward VI and Elizabeth I, began introducing Protestant bishops, bibles and prayer books. Most Irish people refused to accept the English religion or English rule. In Elizabeth's reign, the provinces of Ulster and Munster rose in rebellion. Munster was in a state of rebellion almost continuously from 1566 to 1583. An even more serious uprising occurred in 1595 when Hugh

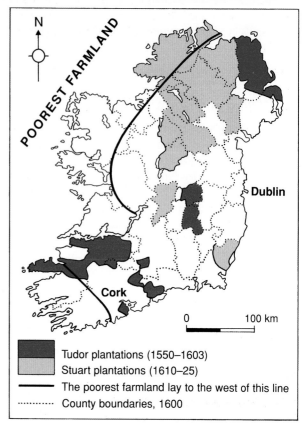

The coming of the Protestants: the Tudor and Stuart Plantations.

Map legend:
- Tudor plantations (1550–1603)
- Stuart plantations (1610–25)
- The poorest farmland lay to the west of this line
- County boundaries, 1600

O'Neill, the Earl of Tyrone, led the people of Ulster in a war against English rule. O'Neill had many early successes and tried to free the whole of Ireland from Tudor power. Eventually the English forces got the upper hand and O'Neill and his Spanish allies were defeated at the Battle of Kinsale in 1601. O'Neill himself survived but was finally forced to surrender in 1603. O'Neill was treated leniently by the English but in 1607 he fled the country.

The Protestant plantations

The English rulers decided that military force alone was not enough to gain control in Ireland. Land was still the main source of power. As long as the land in Ireland stayed in the hands of Catholic nobles, they would still be able to raise the men, horses and supplies to rebel. So the English decided to try a different approach. They would 'plant' colonies of loyal Protestants and give land to them. Plantation had been tried in the 16th century in various parts of Ireland, but these early settlements had not been successful. The flight of O'Neill and his followers in 1607 provided a new opportunity for a plantation in Ulster. From 1610 the land of these Catholic nobles was seized and granted to Protestant settlers.

Irish chieftains fighting, an English view 1581.

Some of the settlers were supporters of the Church of England, known as Anglicans. Others were Scottish Protestants, sometimes known as Presbyterians or Dissenters. The Scots disagreed with Anglican ways but were still loyal to the king. To this day, the Protestants of Ulster remain divided into Anglicans and Presbyterians.

Catholic Rebellion

The Catholics of Ulster felt angry and cheated by the plantations. In 1641 they took part in a great rebellion against the new settlers. Large numbers of Protestants were killed and the rebellion continued until the arrival of the English leader, Oliver Cromwell, in 1649. Cromwell was determined to teach the Irish Catholics a lesson. He did this by slaughtering the Catholic inhabitants of two towns, Drogheda and Wexford. Afterwards he confiscated the lands of the Catholic rebels and drove many of them into the poor western province of Connacht. The rebellion was over but it has never been forgotten. For centuries afterwards Protestants in Ulster feared attacks from their Catholic neighbours. Catholics today still talk about the cruelties of Cromwell.

SOURCE 1

Driuinge Men Women & children by hund: reds vpon Briges & cafting them into Riuers, who drowned not were killed with poles & fhot with mufkets.

G

A Protestant artist's view of the massacre of Portadown Bridge, 1641.

SOURCE 2

The outbreak of the rebellion in 1641 had been marked by the massacre or death from starvation of about 12,000 Scottish and English planters. This was not part of a deliberate plan. Many times Catholic priests intervened to save planters' lives.

A historian's view of the 1641 rebellion: John Ranelagh, *A Short History of Ireland*, 1983.

SOURCE 3

In 1641 the Roman Catholic Church decided to exterminate the Protestants in Ulster and there took place one of the most bloody massacres in Irish history. It was led by the priests of the Roman Catholics and the rivers of Ulster ran red with Protestant blood. The River Bann was so choked with Protestant bodies, that the Roman Catholics could walk dry-shod across the river.

A Protestant politician's interpretation of the 1641 Rising: Ian Paisley, September 1969.

❖ *How do these sources differ?*

The Ulster Plantation: a turning point

The plantation of Ulster was a major turning point along the road to today's conflict in Ireland. Unlike earlier invaders, these new settlers and their descendants kept apart from the Gaelic people. They retained their Protestant religion and their English language. They despised and feared the native Irish. They remained loyal to their rulers in England.

After the Plantation there were two separate hostile 'communities' in Ulster: the descendants of the Protestant British settlers and the native Irish Catholics. From the beginning, their differences were not just about religion but also about political and economic power. As Protestant settlers increased their hold on land and power, so the Gaelic Catholics lost it.

SOURCE 4

The idea that Ireland must be ruled as one unit is totally false. Northern Ireland is utterly different from the Republic of Ireland. This reality has existed for 400 years. It dates from 'The Ulster Plantation' in the early years of the 17th century. These settlers brought with them a way of life which was totally different to that in the rest of Ireland. From that moment the Province of Ulster developed its own way of life. To this day this difference continues.

'Irish unification — Never', a pamphlet by the Democratic Unionist Party, 1984.

❖ *Make a timeline of the important changes that took place in Ireland 1500–1650?*

❖ *What links are there between the Plantations of the 17th century and Ireland today?*

THE PROTESTANT TAKEOVER 1690 – 1770

Despite Cromwell's victory, the Protestant hold on power in Ireland was not yet firm. When Catholic James II became king in 1685, the Protestants began to fear that their land – and their power – would be given back to the Catholics. Even when James was overthrown by Protestants in 1688, their position was not safe. Within a year James had landed in Ireland with an army of French troops. He planned to use Ireland as a base to invade England to regain his throne. This was the kind of situation English rulers had feared since the time of the Spanish Armada.

The Battle of the Boyne: a turning point

The hopes of James and the Irish Catholics were dashed in 1690. The new Protestant king, William of Orange, followed James to Ireland with his own army and defeated him at the Battle of the Boyne on 11 July 1690. After 1690 Protestants made sure they had complete control of Ireland. Ulster Protestants still celebrate the Battle of the Boyne today and William of Orange remains one of their heroes.

Protestants prevented any further attempts by Catholics to regain power. More Catholic land was confiscated so that by 1703 Catholics held only 14% of the land in Ireland. Since the right to vote was linked to land ownership the Irish Parliament was now controlled by Protestants, mostly Anglican landlords.

The Penal Laws

Between 1697 and 1727 the Irish Parliament passed special laws known as the Penal Laws. These remained in force until the end of the 18th century. The table opposite shows the impact of the Penal Laws on the Catholics of Ireland. The Anglican ruling class feared the Catholic population of Ireland but was also suspicious of Presbyterian Dissenters, resenting their control of the two main towns in Ulster, Derry and Belfast. In 1704 the Dissenters were prevented from holding public offices or sitting on town councils unless they agreed to worship in an Anglican church.

Throughout the 18th century the Anglican ruling class controlled everything that mattered in Ireland – even though they were a small minority of the population. This also guaranteed English control of Ireland. Ireland had become yet another colony in the slowly growing British Empire.

❖ *Why was the Battle of the Boyne an important turning-point in Irish history?*
❖ *Explain how the Penal Laws worked.*

PROTESTANT SETTLER LANDOWNERS GAINED POWER

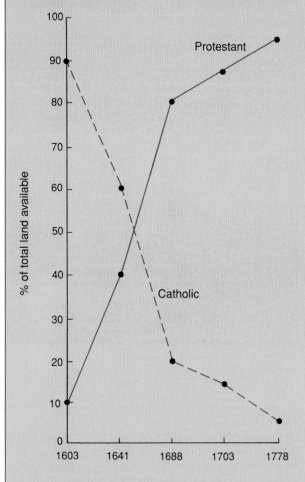

Percentage of land held by Catholics and Protestants, 1603 – 1778

THE TWO SIDES OF VICTORY AT THE BOYNE 1690

NATIVE IRISH CATHOLICS LOST POWER

The Penal Laws 1697-1727

Whereas it is known that past rebellions have been contrived by Popish clergy.
Be it enacted that ....

1. No Catholic may bequeath his lands as a whole but must divide it amongst his sons. But if one of these sons becomes Protestant he will inherit the whole estate. No Catholic can buy land or lease it for more than 31 years.	Because we are Catholics
	We have lost ownership of our land. Now we are only tenants
2. No Catholic shall be allowed to vote or become a member of Parliament or a town councillor. No Catholic shall join the civil service. No Catholic may be a solicitor or lawyer.	We cannot work peacefully to change these laws
3. No Catholic may join the army or the navy No Catholic may possess a horse of greater value than £5. Any Protestant offering that sum may take possession of a horse of his Catholic neighbour. Catholics keeping guns are liable to a whipping.	We cannot fight to get our lands back
4. Catholics may not receive higher education or take professional jobs.	We cannot improve our position in other ways **WHERE DO WE GO FROM HERE?**

REVOLUTIONARY NATIONALISTS 1790 – 1914

The British remained firmly in control of Ireland for a hundred years after the Battle of the Boyne. From the 1790s onwards, groups of Irish people began a struggle to free Ireland from British rule. They wanted the Irish to become an independent 'nation', and they are known as Nationalists. As in the 1790s, Nationalists in Northern Ireland today want the whole of Ireland to be free of British rule.

There have long been two strands in Nationalism:
● Nationalists who believe in the use of peaceful methods;
● Nationalists who are prepared to use violence.

Violent or revolutionary Nationalism developed at the end of the 18th century. Some Irish people were influenced by the revolutions in America and France: between 1775 and 1789 ordinary people in these two countries had overthrown their kings and set up new governments. Revolutionary Nationalists decided that Irish people also needed a new system of government which would be:

INDEPENDENT – free from all ties with the British Empire

DEMOCRATIC – chosen by the majority of the Irish people

REPUBLICAN – without a king.

The first revolutionary organisation was a group called the United Irishmen, founded in 1791. Its founding members were Protestants. One of the leading members of the United Irishmen was a Protestant lawyer called Wolfe Tone. He is still looked upon as a hero by modern Republicans.

SOURCE 1

Wolfe Tone: Sinn Féin supporters view him today as a great hero

Failed rebellions

Revolutionary Nationalists tried to organise armed rebellions on several occasions:
● 1798 The rebellion of Wolfe Tone and the United Irishmen
● 1848 The Young Ireland Revolt
● 1867 The Fenian uprising.
Each of these rebellions had little support from ordinary Irish people and were quickly put down by the British. After Wolfe Tone's rebellion in 1798, the British decided to abolish the Irish parliament. From 1800 Irish MPs had to sit in the British Parliament. All decisions about Ireland were now made in Westminster.

SOURCE 2

My aim was to break the connection with England and win independence. To do this we had to forget past differences and replace the words 'Protestant' and 'Catholic' with the one name of 'Irishman'.

Adapted from Wolfe Tone's autobiography, 1798.

The Fenian tradition

Revolutionary Nationalism was given a new lease of life by the Great Famine of 1845–49. There was a disastrous attempt to organise an armed uprising in 1848. Many Irish people fled to the USA to avoid starvation. They took with them feelings of anger and bitterness towards the British government. In 1858 two secret organisations were set up to plan for a revolution in Ireland: they were called the Fenian Brotherhood and the Irish Republican Brotherhood (IRB). Both groups relied heavily on support from America. From this time onwards revolutionary Nationalists were often referred to as Fenians. A Fenian rebellion in 1867 was easily suppressed by the British forces. After 1867 the Fenians realised there was little support for armed uprisings and instead began to help poor farmers in their fight against harsh landlords. In the 1880s the IRB organised a 'Land League' to stop landlords evicting tenants for not paying their rent. This was successful, forcing the British government to change the land laws.

The Rise of Sinn Féin

In 1905 a new political party was set up, called Sinn Féin (meaning 'Ourselves Alone'). It was led by Arthur Griffith. He wanted Ireland to become independent but he did not plan to achieve this by force. Instead he suggested that the Irish MPs should simply 'opt out' of the British parliament and set up their own government in Dublin. This would collect its own taxes and make its own laws. British rule in Ireland ignored by the majority of the people, would eventually wither away.

Before 1914 both Sinn Féin and the IRB appeared to have little chance of success. Like the earlier revolutionary Nationalists, they still had little support from most people. Without this popular support for the Nationalist cause the British were unlikely to hand over control of Ireland.

SOURCE 4

A magazine illustration showing the murder of two senior British officials by the IRB in Phoenix Park, Dublin, 1882.

SOURCE 3

Members of the Land League burning the leases of a big landowner, 1881.

THE RISE OF THE PARLIAMENTARY NATIONALISTS 1820–1914

Unlike revolutionary Nationalists, parliamentary or constitutional Nationalists have always opposed the use of violence. They began their peaceful campaign for Irish self-rule after the defeat of Wolfe Tone and the abolition of the Irish Parliament in 1800. Another contrast with the republicans was that parliamentary Nationalists did not demand complete independence from Britain. They were willing to remain within the British Empire as long as the Irish people could have a separate parliament again: although this time it had to represent Catholics as well as Protestants. While the revolutionaries suffered defeat after defeat, the parliamentary Nationalists made steady progress during the 19th century.

Daniel O'Connell wins support

The first Nationalist successes were the work of Daniel O'Connell. Between 1820 and his death in 1847, O'Connell was responsible for two important developments:

1. He won the backing of Catholic bishops and priests for the Nationalist cause. They were the one group of people who had contact with ordinary Catholics throughout Ireland. With their help, O'Connell persuaded thousands of Catholics to support his campaign for a separate Irish Parliament.

2. With thousands of Irish voters supporting him, O'Connell was able to force the British government to change the law banning Catholic MPs in 1829. O'Connell's supporters could now go on to build up a party of Irish Nationalist MPs in the British House of Commons. This was important if they were to change the Act of Union which had abolished the old Irish Parliament in 1800.

Daniel O'Connell believed in Irish Nationalism, but was opposed to the use of violence.

Parnell and the campaign for Home Rule

Parnell is ejected from Parliament after disrupting proceedings.

It took a long time to build up an Irish Nationalist Party. By 1885, however, there were 85 Nationalist MPs in Westminster led by a man called Charles Stewart Parnell. Nationalist MPs were now a big enough group to make the two British parties, the Liberals and the Conservatives, take notice of their demands.

Parnell made full use of the new-found power of the Irish Nationalist Party. In the 1880s he joined forces with the Fenians of the Land League who were fighting to protect poor Irish farmers from harsh landlords. Their 'Land War' alarmed British leaders and won sympathy from many ordinary British voters. In Parliament, Parnell demanded changes in the land laws. Between 1881 and 1885 new laws were passed forbidding evictions and high rents and offering tenants loans so they could buy back their land.

After this, in 1886, the leaders of the Liberal Party agreed to help Parnell and the Nationalists in their attempt to set up an Irish Parliament. They brought a 'Home Rule for Ireland' Bill before the House of Commons. Home Rule would have involved the setting up of a parliament in Ireland with limited powers. This was defeated twice – in 1886 and again in 1893. Too many British MPs, including some

Liberals, distrusted the Nationalists. They feared that Home Rule would be the first step towards complete independence for Ireland. At this time British wealth and power depended on her world-wide trade with her empire. An independent Ireland, hostile to Britain and controlling her sea routes, would be a danger to British power.

John Redmond comes close to victory

Parnell's campaign for an Irish parliament was carried on after 1900 by a new leader, John Redmond. He kept up pressure on Liberal leaders after they returned to government in 1906. At long last, in 1912, the Liberals brought a third Home Rule bill before the House of Commons. This time, after two years of debate, the bill was passed. By autumn 1914, Irish people were set to have their own parliament again in Dublin. It looked as if, after nearly 100 years, the Parliamentary Nationalists had triumphed.

❖ *What part did the following people play in the development of Irish Nationalism:*
  ● *Wolfe Tone* ● *Daniel O'Connell* ● *Charles Stuart Parnell* ● *John Redmond?*
❖ *How successful was revolutionary Nationalism in the period 1790–1914?*

19

THE RISE OF UNIONIST OPPOSITION 1790 – 1914

The hopes of the Irish Nationalist Party were dashed by the fierce opposition of Ulster Protestants. In the 18th century the first Irish people to demand independence from Britain had been Protestants: Wolfe Tone and his United Irishmen. Tone had wanted Catholics and Protestants to join together to build a new, fairer system of government for all Irish people. In the 19th century things changed and Protestants became less likely to support Nationalism. Many Protestants became frightened by the idea of a new Irish government dominated by Catholics. They started to worry that they might lose their lands and power if the Nationalists got their way. Protestants began to see all Nationalists – parliamentary or revolutionary – as their enemies. The British – and particularly the British parliament – were now their friends and protectors. The northern province of Ulster was the only part of Ireland where there was a large concentration of Protestants. Ulster, and particularly the Belfast area, did very well out of the Industrial Revolution of the 19th century. Ulster Protestants began to fear that moves towards independence would undermine their prosperity.

The Ulster Unionist Party

Protestant Unionists began to organise themselves to safeguard their position. Some Protestants joined the Orange Order. This was a semi-secret society set up in 1795. It celebrated William of Orange's victory at the Battle of the Boyne and aimed to keep power in Protestant hands. The Orange Order remains a powerful force in Northern Ireland today.

In the 1880s there was a great increase in Protestant fears for the future. Parnell and the Irish Nationalist Party had forced the British government to change the land laws. Next it looked as if they would win Home Rule for Ireland. Protestants now decided the time had come to put a stop to all ideas of an independent Irish parliament. So they set up their own political party to fight to keep Britain and Ireland united. This was the 'Ulster Unionist Party'. By themselves the Ulster Unionists might not have stopped Home Rule. However, in 1886 the British Conservative Party decided to support them. Lord Randolph Churchill, a leading Conservative, urged Ulster Protestants to take up arms if Home Rule became law. 'Ulster will fight and Ulster will be right' was his slogan.

SOURCE 1

Orange Order members marching in the Ormeau Road area of Belfast, 1995.

Ulster will fight!

Support from British Conservatives and some members of the Liberal Party ensured that the Home Rule Bill was defeated in 1886 and another Home Rule Bill was again thrown out in 1893. In 1912, however, the Nationalists seemed certain to win. So, led by a lawyer called Edward Carson, Ulster Protestants organised themselves to fight. Over 400,000 Protestants signed a 'Solemn Covenant' promising to resist a Home Rule parliament in Ireland. They then set up their own private army, the Ulster Volunteers. Within a year they had 100,000 men and £1 million which they used to buy arms from Germany. Carson and the Unionists were given full support by the British Conservative Party. The stand of the Ulster Protestants marked an important development in Irish politics. Home Rule was no longer a certainty. It all depended on whether the British government was prepared to force Protestants to accept a Dublin Parliament against their will.

SOURCE 2

I solemnly swear that I will support and defend the present King George III and all the heirs of the Crown – so long as they support the Protestant ascendancy [hold on power]. I do further swear that I am not, nor ever was, a Roman Catholic or Papist; that I was not, nor never will be a United Irishman and that I never took an oath of secrecy to that Society.

The original oath of the Orange Order, 1795.

SOURCE 4

Edward Carson, shown in a poster to promote the 'Solemn Covenant', 1912.

❖ *Why did Protestants begin to reject Nationalism in the 19th century?*
❖ *Why was the Ulster Unionist Party set up in 1886?*
❖ *What part did Edward Carson play in the fight against Home Rule?*

Ulster Unionist propaganda. John Bull, representing Britain, holds on to Ulster with a rope.

THE IRISH REVOLUTION 1914 – 21

SOURCE 1

Decorations in Dublin for the visit of the British royal family, 1911. Does a Nationalist rising look likely?

By 1914 there were serious problems in Ireland:

● The parliamentary Nationalists had been promised Home Rule by autumn 1914 but the Unionists were determined to stop Ulster being ruled by an all-Ireland parliament.

● Both sides had strong support: the Nationalist Party among Ireland's Catholic voters, the Unionists among the Protestants of Ulster.

● Both sides had private armies. The Unionists had recruited 100,000 Ulster Volunteers in 1912 to fight against Home Rule. In 1913 the Nationalist Party, with the help of a group of Fenians, formed a rival army to fight for Home Rule. They were called the Irish Volunteers. Within a year 75,000 Catholics had joined and they too were smuggling arms in from Germany.

The British government knew that Ireland was close to civil war.

SOURCE 2
Irish Volunteers, 1914.

IRISH NATIONAL VOLUNTEERS' GUN-RUNNING COUP AT HOWTH CO. DUBLIN.

Saved by the war?

The outbreak of the First World War in August 1914 brought a temporary end to the crisis. Redmond and the Nationalist Party agreed that the problem of Home Rule could be set on one side until the end of the war. They thought that the war would not last long. They hoped that after the war Britain would force the Protestants of Ulster to accept a Dublin Parliament. Unionists were beginning to talk about partition – dividing Ireland in two. Nationalists could not accept the idea of partition. As Redmond declared:

'Irish Nationalists can never agree to the mutilation of the Irish nation. Ireland is a unit. The two-nation idea is an abomination.'

Most of the Irish Nationalists accepted the delay to Home Rule and many thousands of Irish men (Catholics as well as Protestants) joined the British army to fight for King and Empire.

The Easter Rising

While many moderate Nationalists were prepared to join the British army, revolutionary Nationalists saw the war as a chance to stage an armed uprising. In 1916, when the war was going badly for Britain, a small group of Fenians organised a rebellion in Dublin on Easter Monday. They took over the General Post Office and proclaimed Ireland an independent Republic. Sinn Féin had nothing to do with the rising but people talked about the rebels as 'Sinn Féiners'. The rebels got little support from ordinary Catholics who were angry at the damage and shootings. After a week of violence the rebels surrendered. Some were executed without a proper trial. News of the executions caused a wave of horror among the Catholic population of Ireland. There was an upsurge of support for Sinn Féin.

For Ulster Unionists the Easter Rising seemed proof that Nationalists were traitors who could not be trusted. Modern Unionists also look back to 1916 as the year when thousands of Ulster men were killed during the Battle of the Somme. In contrast to the Easter Rising the 'sacrifice of the Somme' seemed proof of the loyalty of the Unionist community.

SOURCE 3

A recruiting poster from the First World War.

23

THE TRIUMPH OF SINN FÉIN 1918

In 1918 the war ended. Throughout Britain and Ireland a general election was held. Irish voters had a choice of three different futures for Ireland:

1. Home Rule, but as part of the British Empire (Redmond and the Nationalist Party).

2. British rule for Ireland (Unionists).

3. Complete independence (Sinn Féin and the Revolutionary Nationalists).

The overall winners were Sinn Féin. The Nationalist Party won only a handful of seats. This was an important turning point in Irish history. For a hundred years the majority of Irish Catholic voters had rejected the revolutionaries and supported the parliamentary Nationalists. Now they had a dramatic change of heart. The revolutionary Nationalists had won at last. They lost no time in putting their plans into action. The new Sinn Féin MPs refused to go to London. Instead they declared Ireland an independent Republic and set up their own parliament, the Dáil, in Dublin. They also set up a government, police and law courts.

Shortly afterwards the Irish Volunteers were reorganised and renamed 'The Irish Republican Army' (IRA), under the leadership of Michael Collins, an able organiser who rapidly became expert in guerrilla warfare.

'Men of the South', a painting of IRA men by Sean Keating, 1920. Whose side do you think the artist was on?

The War of Irish Independence 1919–21

On 21 January 1919 the IRA killed two policemen in County Tipperary. This was the start of a two-year guerrilla war fought against British forces in Ireland. Fighting intensified in 1920 and the British government lost control over much of the countryside of southern Ireland. The situation was different in the north. Ulster Protestants wanted no part in a separate Ireland so they gave full support to the British.

In the end neither side got what it wanted. The British government decided that the only solution was to divide Ireland into two parts:

The North

In 1920 the six most Protestant counties of Ulster were given their own parliament and their own government. There was a large Catholic minority in the six counties and in two of the counties there were more Catholics than Protestants. This new government of Northern Ireland became known as Stormont after the district of Belfast where it eventually met. Stormont was to have power over most aspects of life in the North but the new state was to stay part of the UK.

The South

Irish Nationalists were opposed to the idea of dividing Ireland. But in 1921 a group of leading Sinn Féin and IRA members went to London to talk with the British government. In December 1921 they signed a treaty with the British accepting, at least temporarily, the division of Ireland. The 26 counties of southern Ireland became known as the Irish Free State. This was an independent country but initially it remained, like Canada and Australia, part of the British Commonwealth.

The partition of Ireland into two separate states was the most important turning point in recent Irish history. For some time the Irish people had been split into two opposing power groups: Protestant Unionists and Catholic Nationalists. Now their country had been split into two parts: North and South. The partition of Ireland lies at the heart of the modern argument about the future of Ireland.

❖ *What was the impact of the First World War on the crisis in Ireland?*
❖ *What happened during the Easter Rising?*
❖ *Why was Sinn Féin so successful in the 1918 elections?*
❖ *How did Ireland come to be divided in two?*

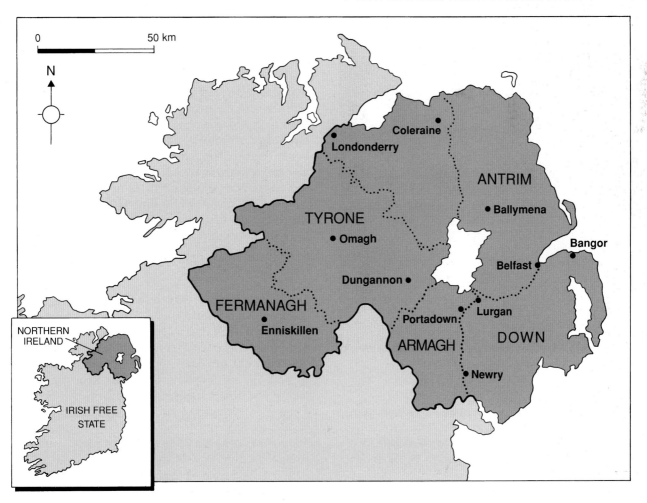

DRIFTING APART

When the Partition Treaty was signed in 1921, both British and Sinn Féin leaders saw it as a temporary solution to Ireland's problems. Both hoped that, in time, these problems could be sorted out so that Ireland could become a united country again. This did not happen. Instead, the two parts of Ireland drifted further apart.

After partition, it was hardline Unionists who held power in the North. They were determined to keep Ulster British and Protestant. They tended to see all northern Catholics as possible traitors. As a result Catholics were discriminated against. In the Irish Free State Catholic Nationalists got the majority of jobs in the new government. The southern state did little to win the hearts and minds of Unionists and Protestants. Hardline Nationalists – those who wanted above all to unite Ireland– were in control. There was little chance that the two parts of Ireland would agree to come together again.

Eamon de Valera

SOURCE 2

We shall continue to deny the right of any foreign authority in Ireland. We shall refuse to admit that our country may be carved up by such as authority.

Eamon de Valera, Taoiseach (Prime Minister) of Ireland.

The South – building a separate state

The 1921 Partition Treaty caused fierce quarrels among Nationalists in the South. The IRA was divided between those who accepted it and those who rejected it. The two sides fought a brutal civil war between 1922 and 1923. It was won by supporters of the treaty. The breach between the two sides took a long time to heal. Since the 1920s there have always been two large political parties in the South: Fianna Fáil and Fine Gael. These parties are descended from the two wings of the IRA that fought the Civil War. Fianna Fáil members originally opposed the treaty, while Fine Gael supported the treaty. For the first ten years supporters of the treaty were in power in the south. Then in the 1932 Irish election they were defeated by Fianna Fáil and their leader Eamon de Valera.

De Valera became the new Taoiseach (Prime Minister) and, with two short breaks, remained in power until 1959. De Valera was born in New York and brought to Ireland as a child by his mother. He was fiercely opposed to any British control in Ireland. He had fought in the Easter Rising in 1916 and he was almost executed by the British. When he came to power in 1932, de Valera was determined to build a strong and independent state in the South. De Valera was a very devout Catholic and he strengthened the role of the Catholic Church in the new state. The table on the page opposite shows what he did in power.

Basil Brooke

SOURCE 1

This country is as determined as in the past to remain part of the UK. Our country is in danger. Today we fight to defend the heritage of our Ulster children. No surrender! We are King's men.

Basil Brooke, Unionist Prime Minister of Northern Ireland 1943–63.

Opponents of the Partition Treaty take to the streets at the start of the bitter civil war.

De Valera's Free State

A united Ireland
In 1937 he introduced a new constitution. This called for a united Ireland and said that Northern Ireland had no right to exist.

A Catholic Ireland
The new constitution also gave a 'special position' to the Catholic Church. Government policy on divorce, the family and education were all in line with Catholic teaching.

A Gaelic Ireland
Great efforts were made to persuade people to speak Gaelic as their main language without success. Ireland remains largely English-speaking.

A free Ireland
De Valera began cutting all remaining economic and political ties with Britain.
• Imports were cut back but it was not so easy to find other markets for Irish goods
• During the Second World War Ireland remained neutral.
• In 1937 the British King was replaced by an Irish president as head of state.
• In 1949 (when de Valera was out of power) the Irish Republic was proclaimed and the country left the British Commonwealth.

SOURCE 4

The Dublin government removes an enormous statue of Queen Victoria, 1949.

❖ Who was Eamon de Valera and what impact did he have on the new state in the south of Ireland?
❖ Why do you think that few Northern Protestants were impressed by developments in the south of Ireland after Partition?

27

ORANGEMEN RULE THE NORTH

Partition also brought problems for people living in the North. Although Protestant Unionists were in the majority, there were still thousands of Catholic Nationalists living there. Many refused to accept the split. Between July 1920 and July 1922 there was fierce street fighting in Belfast and 453 people were killed. This increased Protestant fears about Catholic Nationalists and their links with the South.

Northern Ireland had been given its own parliament. In theory this was meant to look after the interests of the Catholics as well as the Protestants. However, since the Protestants were in the majority, they had control of the Stormont Parliament and the government. Before 1969 every member of the Northern Ireland cabinet was a Protestant and almost all were also members of the Orange Order. Unionists also altered local government election boundaries so that they could win control of local councils as well. This fixing of boundaries is called gerrymandering. The most notorious example of gerrymandering was in Derry. In 1966 10,000 Protestants were able to elect more councillors than 20,000 Catholics.

Protestant Unionists used their political power to help their own community. Catholics found it difficult to get good jobs and decent council houses. They also felt they were treated unfairly by the police. The Northern Ireland government introduced new laws and a new part-time police force as a defence against the IRA. These police, known as the 'B' Specials, were armed and entirely Protestant. They soon gained a reputation for being anti-Catholic.

John Bull and Britannia leaving Northern Ireland (the baby) in the hands of the Unionists (the babysitter). Cartoon from Dublin paper.

What the Unionists thought...

Partition is better than a united Ireland. We will try to make Northern Ireland work to our advantage.

The Catholics cannot be trusted they are traitors to Northern Ireland. As our PM Basil Brooke says "Our country is in danger. No surrender! We are King's men!"

We must keep control of Stormont. As Lord Craigavon put it "We are a Protestant parliament for a Protestant people."

Traitors must not be allowed to run local councils. We must fix boundaries so that Unionists always win.

The new police force needs to keep a close check on Catholic traitors.

We must keep the support of loyal Protestants – they must be given good jobs... and good houses of course – in different parts of town.

Partition: the effects in the North

What the Nationalists thought...

STREET FIGHTING IN THE NORTH BETWEEN CATHOLICS AND PROTESTANTS 1922–23	Partition is wrong. We will have nothing to do with "Northern Ireland". We will not have anything to do with the new government.
UNIONISTS KEEP CONTROL OF STORMONT PARLIAMENT	We will not join the new civil service or police force. We will "opt out" of life in the north just like the south opted out of the UK in 1919.
UNIONISTS KEEP CONTROL OF LOCAL COUNCILS BY 'FIXING' OR GERRYMANDERING' THE ELECTION BOUNDARIES. 8 ELECTED NATIONALIST COUNCILLORS DERRY 1966 12 ELECTED UNIONIST COUNCILLORS	These gerrymandered elections are a farce. Unionists do not want democracy.
UNIONISTS SET UP 'B' SPECIALS — A NEW ARMED PROTESTANT POLICE FORCE AND PASS THE SPECIAL POWERS ACT	The Protestant police force is always picking on innocent Catholics.
UNIONISTS KEEP CONTROL OF JOBS FOR THE PROTESTANTS	Catholics are unfairly discriminated against. Protestants get all the jobs – while we stay unemployed.
UNIONISTS KEEP CONTROL OF COUNCIL HOUSES AND GIVE THE BEST TO PROTESTANTS	What is there for us in a divided Ireland?

In the early years after Partition Northern Catholics were alienated by Unionist discrimination. They felt there was no place for them in the North and there was no point joining in the government of the province. Unemployment was high and Catholics were much more likely to be out of a job than Protestants.

Hopes of peaceful change 1950–68

By the 1950s, however, the mood of many Catholics was beginning to change. Instead of waiting for a united Ireland, many began to accept that they were part of a separate Northern state for the foreseeable future. They began to hope that their lives could be improved by peaceful, social and economic changes.

This new attitude became clear between 1956 and 1962 when the IRA started a new campaign of violence in the North. It failed mainly because ordinary Catholics were not willing to support the IRA and violence. Many IRA leaders were imprisoned. After this the IRA temporarily abandoned the idea of force as the best way to reunite Ireland. Instead it tried to lessen the gap between Nationalists and Unionists by campaigning for improvements in the wages and living conditions of all working people.

By the early 1960s there were also changes in the attitudes of political leaders in both the North and South. This began in 1959 when de Valera retired as Taoiseach (or Prime Minister) of the Irish Republic. Sean Lemass, the new leader, was less hostile to the Unionists in the North. There were similar changes of leadership in the North. In 1963 the hardline Unionist Prime Minister, Lord Brookeborough (Basil Brooke), was replaced by Terence O'Neill. O'Neill was keen to end unfair treatment of Catholics in Northern Ireland. The new hopeful mood was shown to the world in 1965 when Lemass paid a visit to O'Neill at Stormont. It now seemed possible that Catholics and Protestant could work together make a new and fairer way of life in the North.

It was at this time, when real improvements at last seemed possible, that violence again broke out in Northern Ireland.

❖ *In what ways were Catholics badly treated in Northern Ireland after Partition?*

❖ *Why was there a new optimistic mood in Northern Ireland during the mid-1960s?*

1963–67
New Unionist government promises Catholics fairer treatment

Aug 1969
British troops sent in to keep the peace

Aug 1970
Ordinary Catholics oppose violence and form new political party, the SDLP

Jan 1972
Bloody Sunday – British troops shoot at Civil Rights marchers

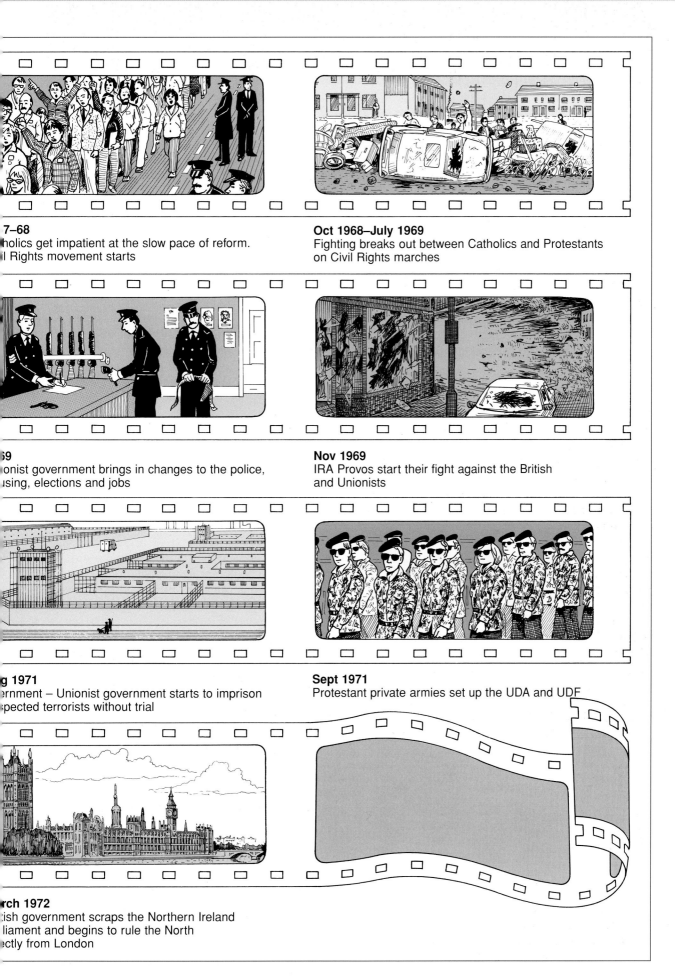

7–68
...holics get impatient at the slow pace of reform.
...l Rights movement starts

Oct 1968–July 1969
Fighting breaks out between Catholics and Protestants
on Civil Rights marches

...69
...onist government brings in changes to the police,
...using, elections and jobs

Nov 1969
IRA Provos start their fight against the British
and Unionists

...g 1971
...rnment – Unionist government starts to imprison
...pected terrorists without trial

Sept 1971
Protestant private armies set up the UDA and UDF

...rch 1972
...ish government scraps the Northern Ireland
...liament and begins to rule the North
...ectly from London

THE NORTH EXPLODES 1968 – 72

Many Northern Catholics originally welcomed O'Neill's talk of a better deal for Catholics but his reforms were too slow in coming and some Catholics became frustrated. So, in 1967 a group of young Catholics got together and set up a Civil Rights Association. This organisation demanded immediate reforms in the way Northern Ireland was run. From October 1968, they organised a series of protest marches. These marches ended in violence and bloodshed between Catholics and Protestants. Civil Rights marchers were opposed by followers of the Protestant preacher, Ian Paisley. The Paisleyites were also unhappy with O'Neill: they thought he was making too many concessions to the Catholics. The mainly Protestant police also took a tough line towards the Civil Rights campaigners.

SOURCE 1

Catholics fight with the police, August 1969.

SOURCE 2

British troops in Northern Ireland, 1969.

O'Neill found it impossible to stop violence spreading and resigned in April 1969. By August 1969 fighting between Catholics and the Protestant police was out of control. The British government stepped in and sent British troops to restore order. British troops were meant to be a short-term emergency measure but they have been there ever since.

The British government also persuaded the Unionist leaders to introduce reforms. These concentrated on four things:

1. **The Police**
   The part-time B Specials were abolished.
   The RUC was brought under army control.
2. **Housing**
   A fairer system of allocating council houses was set up.
3. **Elections**
   Gerrymandering was stopped.
4. **Unemployment**
   British government gave financial grants to set up new industries.

These reforms failed to stop the fighting.

In August 1971, as a last resort, the Stormont government brought in new rules allowing suspected 'terrorists' to be imprisoned without trial. They were kept in internment camps like enemy prisoners in wartime. Internment also failed to stop the fighting.

SOURCE 3

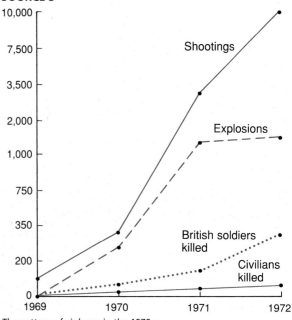

The pattern of violence in the 1970s.

Return of the IRA and UVF

By early 1972 the situation had reached crisis point. The violence in Northern Ireland had gone beyond street fighting and rioting. Private armies had appeared on the streets of Belfast and Derry. After their failure in 1956–62, the IRA were back and now controlled the Catholic streets of these cities. This time there was a new group of young IRA men calling themselves 'The Provisional' IRA (after the provisional government set up in Dublin during the 1916 Easter Rising). The Provisionals had broken away from the old 'Official' IRA in 1969–70 because they disagreed with the policies of its leaders. After this the 'Officials' stayed in the South trying to reunite Ireland by peaceful persuasion of the Catholic and Protestant working classes. The 'Provos' took control of operations in the North, convinced that only force would bring an end to the British occupation of the North. Meanwhile, on the other side of the barricades, were the Protestant paramilitaries, the Ulster Volunteer Force (UVF) and the Ulster Defence Association (UDA). They were determined to fight to keep Ulster British.

Direct Rule 1972

Many people on both sides did not support these private armies. There was widespread support for a purely peaceful approach to politics. In 1970 a group of Catholic Nationalists set up the Social Democratic Labour Party (SDLP) to campaign for peaceful change. The SDLP became the largest Nationalist party but they were not able to stop the violence. It was now clear that the Stormont government had lost all control of the province. With Northern Ireland on the brink of civil war, the British government decided there was only one thing to do. It suspended the Northern Ireland government and parliament and began to rule the province direct from Britain.

The years 1968–72 had brought two more turning points in the history of today's conflict:
● in 1968 hopes of peace between Nationalists and Unionists were dashed by the outbreak of fighting.
● in 1972 the Unionist-controlled government of Northern Ireland, set up in 1921, was suspended.

❖ *What groups in Northern Ireland were unhappy with the government of Terence O'Neill?*
❖ *What is meant by Direct Rule? Why did the British government introduce Direct Rule in 1972?*

SOURCE 4

Graffiti in support of the IRA (Oglaigh na hEireann in Gaelic).

BRITAIN AND IRELAND SINCE 1972

Since 1972 the British government has tried a number of possible solutions to the crisis in Northern Ireland:

1. Power-sharing

In 1974 the British tried to set up a new system of government in which power would be shared between Protestants and Catholics. The leader was Brian Faulkner, leader of the Unionist Party, and his deputy was Gerry Fitt, the leader of the Nationalist SDLP. This 'Power-Sharing' failed after only five months because the Protestants opposed it.

In 1982 the British set up a new Northern Ireland Assembly elected by fair voting. At first this was to have powers of discussion only. But if the Protestants and Catholics could agree to work together on any problem they were able to be given power to deal with it. This also failed. Catholics refused to attend the Assembly.

Brian Faulkner, leader of the Power-Sharing Executive, 1974.

2. Changes in the police and security forces

When British troops were first sent to Ulster in 1969 they were given complete control of all peace-keeping operations and the Royal Ulster Constabulary. Since then the British government has gradually reduced the number of regular soldiers. In 1977 they handed back control to the RUC. Although the RUC was meant to be a 'mixed' police force, by the early 1990s only 7% of its members were Catholic. Throughout the 1970s and 1980s the RUC was supported by the Ulster Defence Regiment (UDR). This was formed from local recruits in 1970 after the notorious Protestant B Specials were disbanded. The UDR was meant to be a mixed regiment but, in fact, 97% of the soldiers were Protestants. Criticism of the UDR led to its amalgamation in 1993 into a new force known as the Royal Irish Regiment.

UDR soldiers on patrol.

3. Rough justice

As well as trying 'Power-Sharing' experiments, the British leaders have also tried to stop the bombings and shootings. To do this they have used tough methods:

- plastic bullets in riots
- trials without juries
- unsupported evidence of informers to convict 'terrorist' suspects
- shooting dead suspected IRA members.

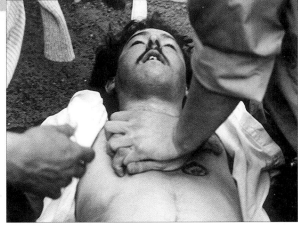

The victim of a plastic bullet.

Talks with Dublin: Garret Fitzgerald and Margaret Thatcher.

4. Talks with the Republic

Since 1980 the British government has also been involved in talks with leaders of the Irish Republic. Leaders in the South believe that the conflict in the North cannot be solved unless they are part of any peace plan. In 1984 they suggested that the only long-term solution was to unite North and South in a single state. This idea was flatly rejected by the British Prime Minister, Margaret Thatcher.

In 1985, however, the British signed 'the Anglo-Irish Agreement' with the Republic. This set up a joint committee of the two governments to discuss such matters as the security forces, justice and the law in Northern Ireland. They hoped to find ways of persuading Unionists and Nationalists to respect each other's rights and views. However, Unionists claimed that for the first time since Partition in 1921, the British was allowing the Government of the Republic a say in the running of the North. Further talks in the 1990s led to the Downing Street Declaration in 1993: a joint statement about the future of Northern Ireland agreed by both the Dublin and the London governments.

❖ *Explain in your own words how the British government has used different methods to try to end the crisis in Northern Ireland since 1972?*
❖ *How successful has the British government been in dealing with Northern Ireland since 1972?*

THE NATIONALIST REACTION SINCE 1972

Since the outbreak of violence in 1968–72, the activities of Unionist extremists and the tough policy of the British made some Northern Nationalists more bitter than ever. Many Catholics once again felt that there could be no place for them in a state controlled by the Unionists or the British. Many once again looked to the idea of a united Ireland as a solution to their problems. However, as in the past there were disagreements among Nationalists about the right methods to use in order to achieve a united Ireland.

The Parliamentary Nationalists

The SDLP, led by John Hume, are the modern Parliamentary Nationalists. Like O'Connell in the 19th century, they want to solve Ireland's problems by peaceful negotiation.

They support the Anglo-Irish agreement because the Irish Republic committee members will be able to speak up on behalf of Northern Nationalists. The SDLP have won friends in Britain but not amongst the IRA.

SOURCE 1

Last week John Hume's election headquarters were burned down. A day earlier an IRA statement described him as 'part of the British war machine'.

Extract from the *Sunday Times*, 6 May 1984.

SOURCE 2

The Revolutionary Nationalists – The IRA

The IRA is the main modern example of Revolutionary Nationalism. Since the early 1970s it has planted bombs in Northern Ireland and in mainland Britain which have killed and injured ordinary civilians, including children. At times the IRA has changed tactics and has put more emphasis on attacking the police, the army and leading British figures. Lord Mountbatten, the Queen's uncle, was murdered in 1979. In 1984 a bomb planted in a Brighton hotel nearly killed the Prime Minister, Margaret Thatcher, and other government members.

SOURCE 3

Thatcher will now realise that Britain cannot occupy our country, torture our prisoners and get away with it. Today we were unlucky. But remember we have only to be lucky once – you have to be lucky always. Give Ireland peace and there will be no war!

The IRA claim responsibility for the Brighton bombing, Irish Republican Press Bureau, October 1984.

The IRA paid great attention to publicity. Between 1976 and 1981 imprisoned IRA men demanded special treatment as political prisoners and refused to wear prison clothes. The British refused to let them have their own clothes, so they wore none at all. They also began a 'dirty protest' — smearing their cells with their own excrement. In 1981 a group of IRA prisoners, led by Bobby Sands, went on hunger strike. Ten of them starved themselves to death. The hunger strikes won great sympathy and strengthened the position of the IRA.

Belfast graffiti gives a different view of the meaning of the letters SDLP.

**The Nationlist debate since 1970:
'How do we get a united Ireland?'**

By peaceful talks?   By prison protests?   By the bomb?   By the 'ballot as well as the bullet'?

Sinn Féin

In the 1980s some of the younger IRA men, led by Gerry Adams, brought forward a new idea. Using the old name Sinn Féin, they decided to build up a new political party for Revolutionary Nationalists in Ireland. Adams argued that it was important to have MPs and local councillors who support the aims of the IRA. This would show the people of Britain and America that ordinary Catholics support the IRA and that it is not just a 'criminal conspiracy'.

In the election of 1983 Adams was elected as British MP for West Belfast, although he refused to take his seat. Sinn Féin went on to do well in local council elections in Northern Ireland. Sinn Féin leaders talked of 'using the ballot as well as the bullet' to win a united Ireland. They wanted Sinn Féin to become the main Nationalist party in the North instead of the SDLP. The threat of Sinn Féin was one factor that led to the Anglo-Irish agreement in 1985. Since then the increase in support for Sinn Féin has tailed off. In the decade after 1985 Sinn Féin regularly won about one third of the Catholic vote in Northern Ireland elections; and the SDLP picked up the remaining two-thirds of Catholic votes.

The Sinn Féin attempt to become the voice of the Nationalist community ultimately failed. Adams himself lost his seat as MP to an SDLP politician in 1992. Throughout the 1980s and the early 1990s Sinn Féin maintained its support, but it was never able to get much more than a third of the overall Catholic/Nationalist vote. Attempts to win support in the Republic were even more disappointing. In elections held in the Republic Sinn Féin was only able to win a minute fraction of the overall vote. Most Nationalists – North and South – preferred to stick with the parties committed to peaceful change.

The IRA continued its campaign of violence but in the late 1980s it experienced a number of disasters. In May 1987 the SAS shot dead eight IRA men as they prepared to attack an RUC station at Loughall. For the IRA this was the single heaviest loss of life in any operation. In November of the same year the IRA exploded a bomb at a Remembrance Parade at Enniskillen, killing eleven people and badly injuring many more. The public in Ireland and Britain were sickened by the killing of so many innocent people at Enniskillen, and there was sense of revulsion about the IRA's activities. In March 1988 three unarmed IRA members were shot dead by the SAS as they undertook an operation in Gibraltar.

With his party support stuck at about a third of the Catholic vote, and with widespread criticism of IRA activities, Gerry Adams began to explore a new policy. He decided to encourage IRA/Sinn Féin to end the armed struggle and use peaceful methods. Having failed to destroy the other Nationalist party, the SDLP, the Sinn Féin leaders considered working with it. In 1988 Adams began talks with John Hume, the SDLP leader. Adams persuaded the IRA to declare a cease-fire in 1994 and again in 1997. Ten long years after the start of the Hume-Adams talks both men supported the 1998 Good Friday Agreement which set up a power-sharing assembly in Northern Ireland. This was a great achievement, but it was not a united Ireland, and some hard-line Nationalists were very unhappy with Adam's policy.

❖
  Why do you think that the SDLP and IRA/Sinn Féin
❖ *have often criticised each other's actions?*
  How did Sinn Féin tactics change after the Hunger Strike of 1981?
❖ *Why did Gerry Adams try to change the direction of Sinn Féin after 1988?*

THE UNIONIST REACTION SINCE 1972

Some Unionists believed that the coming of violence and the revival of the IRA after 1969 was due partly to the weakness of their own leaders. In 1971, a new party called the Democratic Unionist Party (DUP) was set up, led by Ian Paisley. Paisley was well-known for his fiercely anti-Catholic, anti-Nationalist and anti-British government views. The DUP soon challenged the Ulster Unionist Party as the voice of Unionism.

Some extreme Unionists set up Protestant private armies: the Ulster Defence Association (UDA) and the Ulster Volunteer Force (UVF). These organisations specialised in 'sectarian' murders: the killing of innocent Catholics in retaliation for IRA attacks on Protestant policemen and part-time soldiers. While Sinn Féin represents the IRA, no major political party represents the loyalist private armies. Members of the UDA and UVF have occasionally tried to challenge the two big Unionist parties but they have not been able to get much support during elections.

No power-sharing

Since 1972, Unionists have opposed all moves to involve Nationalists in the government of Ulster. In 1974 they wrecked the 'Power-Sharing' system by means of a general strike of all Protestant workers. It lasted a fortnight and brought ordinary life in the province to a halt. Unionists have also consistently objected to the idea that Dublin should get involved in the affairs of Northern Ireland. They also opposed moves to involve Sinn Féin in talks about Northern Ireland, on the grounds that Sinn Féin represented a criminal gang of murderers.

SOURCE 1

If we cannot arrest the IRA and disarm them they are going to kill us. We have not only the right but the duty to kill them before they kill me, my family and others.

The ordinary Ulster man is not going to surrender to the IRA or be betrayed into a united Ireland or put his neck under the jackboot of Popery.

Ian Paisley, January 1982.

SOURCE 2

Ian Paisley, holding a sledgehammer with the words 'Smash Sinn Fein'

SOURCE 3
A Protestant wall-painting with slogans in support of the Protestant paramilitaries.

No links with the South

Unionists were on the defensive throughout the 1980s. At the beginning of the decade they were constantly worried by the talks between the British government and leaders of the Irish Republic.

SOURCE 4

The only thing that Protestants are afraid of is a dirty, underhanded deal done behind our backs. We are in the hands of our English masters. And we understand that they are not our friends. They would like to destroy us. Protestants love their liberty too much to put themselves into a state where there is censorship but no divorce.

Adapted from a speech by Ian Paisley, December 1981.

To Unionists the 1985 Anglo-Irish Agreement was just such a dirty deal. There was a tremendous sense of outrage and betrayal at news of the Agreement. Unionists were incensed that, even though they were the largest group in Northern Ireland, they had not been consulted about the changes. They saw the new powers of consultation for Dublin as a major step towards a British withdrawal and a united Ireland.

Traditionally Unionists had always said that they must never 'give an inch' to Nationalist demands. A a result they saw the Anglo-Irish Agreement as a disaster. The Agreement also confirmed Unionist fears that the British government was not to be trusted.

◆ *Look at the following sources. What can we learn from these extracts about Unionist attitudes towards the Agreement?*

SOURCE 5

This agreement will not bring peace, but a sword. I have to say honestly and truthfully that I have never known what I can only describe as a universal cold fury.

The leader of the Ulster Unionist Party, James Molyneaux, expresses the common Unionist view of the Agreement in November 1985.

SOURCE 6

The hearts of Ulster have been stricken with the deepest of sorrows. Mrs Thatcher tells us that the Republic has got a say in this province. We say never, never, never, never. We are prepared to lay down our lives for Ulster. I never thought I would live to see the day when 1912 was repeated.

Ian Paisley, speaking at a Unionist rally in Belfast, 24 November 1985.

SOURCE 7

Popular Unionism.

SOURCE 8

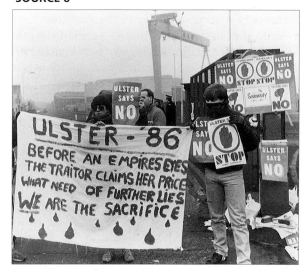

Protestant shipyard workers demonstrate against the Anglo-Irish Agreement.

Unionist frustration

There seemed to be little possibility of peace in Northern Ireland in the late 1980s. Unionists spent much of their energy continuing to denounce the Anglo-Irish Agreement. Throughout 1986 they tried strenuously to overturn the Agreement. In January all the Unionist MPs resigned from the House of Commons and forced by-elections as a sort of referendum about the Agreement. Almost all Protestants voted for anti-Agreement parties. In March there was a Unionist 'day of action'. This was a general strike that closed down much of Northern Ireland. Unionist local councils refused to co-operate with the government. Despite all these protests the government refused to change the Agreement.

The parliamentary Unionists seemed unable to change government policy. Some Protestants turned instead to the loyalist paramilitaries for their security. By 1990 loyalist killers were carrying out an increasing number of random attacks on Catholics. One familiar tactic was to call a taxi from a known Catholic firm and kill the driver. Whenever the IRA staged an attack, Loyalists tended to carry out a reprisal. These 'tit-for-tat' killings reached a climax of horror in 1992–1993. In January 1992 the IRA killed eight Protestant building workers at Teebane, because they were doing work for the security forces. In February the Ulster Freedom Fighters (UFF) responded by killing five Catholics at a betting shop in Belfast. In November, after an IRA bomb had destroyed the shopping centre of the Protestant town of Coleraine, three more Catholics were killed by the UFF in another Belfast betting shop. In March 1993 four Catholic building workers were killed by the UFF as they turned up for work at Castlerock. Later on the same day the UFF killed a Catholic teenager in Belfast. The IRA tried to kill the UFF leaders in October 1993 but only succeeded in blowing up ten

innocent Protestants in a fish and chip shop in Belfast. The Loyalists responded by killing twelve Catholics within a few days: seven in one attack on a bar in Greysteel.

❖ *How did Unionists respond to the Anglo-Irish Agreement of 1985?*
❖ *How successful were Unionist attempts to overthrow the Anglo-Irish Agreement?*
❖ *Explain in your own words how loyalist violence increased in the early 1990s*

SOURCE 5

Unionists were outraged when an IRA bomb killed ten Protestants on the Shankill Road, Belfast, in October 1993.

SOURCE 6

Protestant shipyard workers lead thousands of protesters along the Shankill Road after the October 1993 bombing.

Cease-fire and beyond

By the early 1990s there was apparent stalemate in Northern Ireland:

● Unionists continued to object to the Anglo-Irish Agreement but the British government refused to change the Agreement;

● Sinn Féin had failed in its attempt to overtake the SDLP as the voice of Nationalism;

● The Anglo-Irish Agreement had not diminished support for Sinn Féin;

● IRA violence continued at a high level;

● Loyalist paramilitaries carried out a brutal campaign of sectarian killing.

Underneath the surface some important developments were taking place. Gerry Adams of Sinn Féin and John Hume of the SDLP were engaged in talks about how Nationalists could devise a new peaceful approach to politics in Northern Ireland. There were also secret talks between Sinn Féin and the British government about how Sinn Féin could become involved in negotiations if and when the IRA stopped its campaign of violence. The governments of London and Dublin continued to explore ways of bringing peace to Ireland.

These developments led to an agreement between Adams and Hume in April 1993. The two men informed Dublin that there was a possibility of the IRA ceasing its violence if the British government made it clear how talks could begin about the future of Ireland. The two governments responded by producing the so-called Downing Street Declaration in November 1993. In this the prime ministers of the Republic and the UK stated how they wished to encourage talks among all the people of Ireland. The Declaration made it clear that the British had no wish to remain in Ireland against the wishes of the people (although this included the wishes of the Ulster Unionists). After months of internal debate the IRA announced on 31 August that there would be a cease-fire. Shortly afterwards the loyalist paramilitaries also declared a cease-fire.

The cease-fire did not lead to rapid progress. The British government said that Sinn Féin could play no part in peace talks until the IRA began to hand over weapons. The IRA refused. In February 1996 the IRA ended the cease-fire, and killed two people in London. In 1997 Tony Blair became British Prime Minister, and his new Labour government tried to get peace talks going. The IRA declared a new cease-fire in July 1997, and Sinn Féin was allowed to join the peace talks. Negotiations continued throughout late 1997 and early 1998. On 10 April 1998, Good Friday, a peace deal was agreed. Under the Good Friday Agreement a new power-sharing assembly was given day-to-day control over Northern Ireland.
❖

❖ *Why did the IRA suspend their cease-fire in 1996?*
❖ *How successful has the Good Friday Agreement*
❖ *been in bringing peace to Northern Ireland?*

SOURCE 7

Crowds in Belfast celebrate soon after the declaration of the IRA cease-fire.

1: RELIGION

Today the people of Northern Ireland are divided by many things. One factor separating Nationalists and Unionists is religion. The divide between Catholics and Protestants goes back a long way to the 16th and 17th centuries. It was then that British rulers first brought the Protestant church and Protestant settlers to Ireland.

The overwhelming majority of Northern Protestants are also Unionists. Nearly all Nationalists in Northern Ireland are also Catholics. Does that mean that the religious difference has caused the political divide? Historians think that this is too simple an explanation. There are many places in the world – such as the USA and mainland Britain – where Catholics and Protestants live side by side without any political hostility. The link between religion and politics in Ireland is a complicated one:

- Historically some of the most famous Nationalists have been Protestants – notable examples of Protestant Nationalists include Wolfe Tone and Charles Parnell;

- A minority of Northern Catholics have no wish to live in a united Ireland.

By itself the religious difference cannot explain the conflict in Ireland. The divisions in the north of Ireland are caused by the two communities having a different sense of identity. Religion is one of several reasons why the two groups see themselves as being different from each other and are suspicious of each other. There are many other examples from around the world of this link between religion and identity:

- Bosnia: Bosnian Muslims are in conflict with Bosnian Serbs who belong to the Orthodox Christian Church;

- Sri Lanka: Buddhist Sinhalese are in conflict with Hindu Tamils;

- Israel: Israeli Jews have been involved in a long dispute with their neighbours, the Muslim Palestinians;

- Cyprus: Christian Greek Cypriots disagree strongly with Muslim Turkish Cypriots about the future of their island.

Each of these examples is similar to Northern Ireland in that distinct groups of people live side by side and have different views about how the territory they share should be governed. In each case the dispute has led to violence. Religious differences have encouraged these people to see themselves as being different to their neighbours and have been one barrier to co-operation between them.

An English cartoonist's view of the religious divide in Northern Ireland, *The Guardian*, 1969.

❖ *Can you find any news stories of people of different religions carrying out acts of violence against each other? Are there any similarities or differences with the situation in Northern Ireland?*

How did the connection develop between politics and religion?

1. England 1530s: The King breaks with Rome

Throughout the Middle Ages almost all people in western Europe were Catholics who accepted the Pope in Rome as the leader of the Church. This situation changed during the Reformation of the 16th century. Led by the German, Martin Luther, and the Frenchman, John Calvin, many people rejected the Catholic Church and tried to set up a new 'reformed' Church. These religious rebels were known as Protestants. The Reformation in England began when Henry VIII broke all links between the English Catholic Church and the Pope in Rome during the early 1530s. In 1534 Henry declared himself to be 'Supreme Head' of the Church of England. In 1537 the Irish parliament in Dublin decreed that Henry was 'the only Supreme Head on Earth of the whole Church of Ireland'. Henry took charge of the Church in England and Ireland because the Pope had refused to grant him a divorce from his first wife, Catherine of Aragon. More Protestant ideas were introduced in England and Ireland under Henry's successor, his son, Edward VI. In 1549 the Catholic service of the Mass was banned in Ireland. Irish people were ordered to use a Protestant prayer book. The new prayers were in English, even though most Irish people spoke only Gaelic. Most refused to accept the new Protestant ideas and were angry that they were ordered to pray in a foreign language.

SOURCE 1

King Henry VIII handing out copies of the Bible translated into English.

Some religious differences between Catholics and Protestants

Catholic	*Protestant*
The leader of the Catholic Church is the Pope. He represents Christ on Earth.	The Pope is wrong when he claims to represent Christ. His leadership is rejected.
Services often contain elaborate ritual. Priests have special powers.	Services are simpler. Ministers do not have supernatural powers.
Priests must not marry. Monks and nuns do not marry.	Ministers can marry. Marriage is better than a monastic way of life.
Special veneration is given to the Virgin Mary and other saints.	Little attention is given to saints. The Bible is given special veneration.

2. England 1570: The Pope strikes back

Powerful Catholics, such as the Pope and the King of Spain, were very unhappy at the way the Tudors broke away from the Catholic Church. After a brief interlude when England and Ireland were ruled by the Catholic Mary Tudor (1553–58), the Reformation continued during the long reign of Elizabeth I (1558–1603). The Spanish King, Philip II, and the Pope decided that Elizabeth should be overthrown and replaced with a Catholic monarch. They called upon Catholics in England and Ireland to rebel against her. Pope Pius V issued a papal decree ordering this.

SOURCE 2

We do declare Elizabeth to be cut off from the Holy Catholic Church, and we declare her to be deprived of her pretended title to the kingdom. We command all noblemen and subjects not to obey her or her orders and laws.

The Pope excommunicates Elizabeth I, 1570.

SOURCE 3

3. England and Ireland 1570-1603: Catholic rebellions

By 1570 most of Elizabeth's English subjects were Protestants, so the orders from Rome to rebel meant nothing to them. However, there was a Catholic minority in England and an overwhelming Catholic majority in Ireland. They were in a difficult situation: the government ordered them to do one thing, their Church ordered them to do another. Although many Catholics remained loyal, for the next 30 years Elizabeth faced a series of plots and rebellions in England and Ireland. In 1588 Philip II of Spain sent the Spanish Armada to conquer England. The attempt failed. The most serious rebellion took place in Ireland in 1595–1603. The rebel leader, Hugh O'Neill, said that he was fighting for 'Christ's Catholic Religion'. He was helped by Philip II. In 1601 a Catholic army of 3,500 Spaniards landed in Ireland to reinforce O'Neill. The Catholic forces were defeated by the English at the Battle of Kinsale.

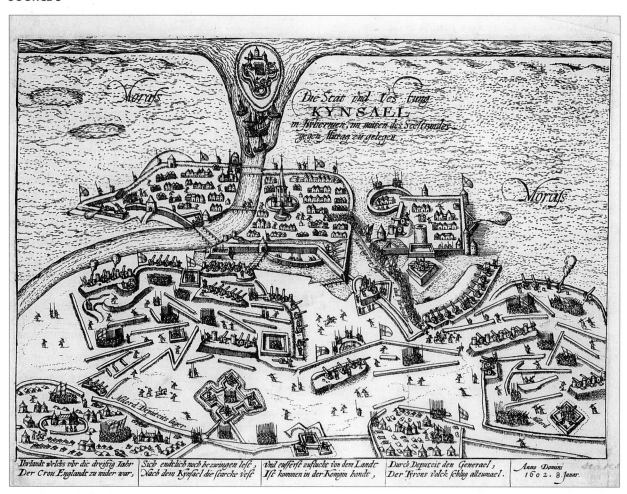

The Battle of Kinsale, 1601

4. Ireland 1608–10: The Plantation of Ulster begins

Despite the failure of the Catholic rebellions Ireland was still a problem for the English government. Most Irish landowners refused to become Protestants. Some were still ready to plot with Spain to get rid of Elizabeth's successor, James I. So James decided to make sure that Irish leaders would in future be loyal subjects of England's Protestant King. He sent loyal Protestant settlers to live in Ireland, especially in the province of Ulster.

5. Ireland 1641–1790: Catholic rebellion and repression

The Catholics of Ulster felt angry and cheated by the loss of their land and power. In 1641 they took part in a great rebellion against the Protestant settlers. Their grievances were political and economic.

Catholics made a further attempt to regain their land during the struggle for the crown in 1688–91. Once again the Catholics failed. The Protestant, William of Orange, defeated the Catholic, James II. This was a great blow to the Catholics of Ireland. Protestants had secured their power in Ireland. They dominated the Irish Parliament and, between 1695 and 1727, they passed a series of laws that discriminated against Catholics.

SOURCE 4

A Protestant picture of Catholics attacking Protestant settlers in the 1641 Rebellion. The writing reads 'English Protestants stripped naked and turned into the mountains in the frost and snow, whereof many hundreds are perished to death and many lying dead in ditches and [the] savages upbraided them saying, "Now are you wild Irish as well as we."'.

SOURCE 5

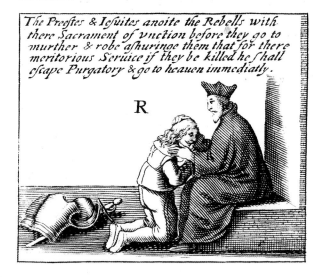

A Protestant's eye-view of the Catholic rebellion, 1641. The writing reads 'The Priests and Jesuits anoint the rebels with their sacrament of unction before they go to murder and rob – assuring them that for their meritorious service if they be killed he shall escape purgatory and go to heaven immediately.'

6. Catholicism and Irish Nationalism 1790–1850

In the 1790s Irish Nationalists began a long fight to free Ireland from British rule. The first Revolutionary Nationalists wanted to keep religion out of this political battle. The pioneers of Nationalism were, for the most part, Irish Protestants who disliked rule from London. Wolfe Tone called upon Irish people of all faiths to unite to fight their common enemy: the English.

SOURCE 6

The people are divided and distrustful of each other. This Society of United Irishmen wishes to create a brotherhood of affection between Irishmen of both religions – Catholics and Protestants.

Wolfe Tone, Revolutionary Nationalist, 1798.

A strong connection between Nationalism and the Catholic Church began to develop in the first half of the 19th century. The Parliamentary Nationalist, Daniel O'Connell, was a Catholic and he wanted to win mass support for his brand of moderate Nationalism. He looked to the Catholic priests of Ireland to help him get support and money from the Catholic majority.

O'Connell set up an organisation called the Catholic Association in 1823 to campaign for political rights for Irish Catholics. He encouraged poor Catholics to join the Association and he used Catholic priests to collect subscriptions.

7. The gulf increases: Ireland 1800–1918

The influence of religion over Irish people grew in the 19th century. At the same time the gulf between the two communities also developed. In Ulster, Protestant preachers, such as Henry Cooke and Hugh Hanna, attacked Catholic teachings and criticised those Protestants who were too easygoing and too soft on the Catholic Church. They taught their congregations that Catholic priests were wicked men who wanted to enslave the people of Ireland. From 1859 there was a great 'revival' of Protestantism in Ulster. Large numbers of people flocked to the Protestant churches of the province. At the same time there was an upsurge of devotion among the Catholics of Ireland. In the middle of the 19th century the powerful leader of the Catholics of Ireland, Cardinal Paul Cullen, urged Catholics to have as little to do with Protestants as possible. He boasted that he had never eaten a meal with a Protestant. Protestants were alarmed by the new power and discipline of the Catholic Church under Cullen.

Protestants in the late 19th century feared the power that Catholic bishops might have in an independent Ireland. This encouraged them to support Unionism. Protestant fears increased further in 1907 when Pope Pius X announced that mixed marriages of Catholics and Protestants would only be allowed if the Protestant parent agreed that the children would be brought up as Catholics. To the Protestant minority in Ireland this seemed like a recipe for their gradual extermination. In each generation there would be more Catholic children and fewer Protestant ones.

SOURCE 7

A 19th-century Protestant cartoon showing Erin (Ireland) bound in ropes by a Catholic priest.

8. North and South since 1920

Since 1920 Ireland has been divided into two parts; the South, controlled by Catholic Nationalists and the North which has a majority of Protestant Unionists. The old mixture of religious and political fears has continued to cause conflict. Religion has remained a powerful force throughout Ireland. Some Protestants, such as Ian Paisley, continue to see the Catholic Church as a wicked organisation that wishes to enslave free Protestants. Most Protestants, including many who have voted for Paisley, do not share these extreme views. The Catholic Church has been a dominant force in the south of Ireland since partition. In recent years many people, particularly in the large city of Dublin, have come to reject the authority of the Church. Despite these changes Unionists have remained unimpressed by the way the Catholic Church has influenced aspects of life in the Republic of Ireland. They continue to fear the power of the Catholic bishops and priests in a united Ireland.

SOURCE 8

Nuns in the Irish Republic voting during government referendums on changing the laws on divorce and abortion, both opposed by the Catholic Church.

❖ *How did the religious changes of the 16th century increase suspicion between Irish people and the London government?*

❖ *Why did the British government send Protestants to Ireland during the plantation of the 17th century?*

❖ *What part did the following people play in creating a gulf between Catholics and Protestants:*
  ● *Henry Cooke and Hugh Hanna*
  ● *Paul Cullen.*

❖ *Why were many Protestants unhappy at the way the Catholic Church approached mixed marriages?*

❖ *How has religion contributed to mistrust between Catholics and Protestants in the 20th century?*

❖ *Look at the following sources. How do these sources help us to explain why some Protestants do not want to be ruled from Dublin?*

SOURCE 9

The influence of the Catholic Church on daily life in the South

1925   Divorce banned in the new Southern state.

1929   Censorship Board established to 'obscene' books and those recommending contraception.

1937   New constitution recognises 'special position' of Catholic Church (withdrawn in 1972 as a concession to Protestants).

1951   Bishops stop new health care system for mothers and babies.

1979   Contraceptives legalised, but only for married couples with a doctor's prescription.

1983   Anti-abortion clause written into the constitution, after a referendum.

1986   Referendum on divorce rejects any change in the law.

1995   Another referendum on divorce overturns the law and approves divorce.

SOURCE 10

You see the Roman Catholic Church is the anti-Christ. There isn't really a political solution, because its a religious battle against the rising of the anti-Christ.

Mrs Hamilton, a Presbyterian Dissenter and supporter of Ian Paisley, speaking in 'Only rivers run free', 1984.

❖ *Look at the following sources. What can we learn from these sources about why some Protestants distrust the power of the Catholic Church?*

SOURCE 11

We must recognise the genuine fears of the Northern Protestant that in a united Ireland he would be in a minority and that he would suffer in much the same way as the Catholic minority in Ulster. There is the position of the Catholic Church. There are the Catholic rules on mixed marriages, the right to contraception and family planning, the right to divorce. There is the question of social services. In the north they have better health services, unemployment benefits and old age pensions.

Adapted from a speech by Noel Browne, Irish Labour Party, 1971.

SOURCE 12

It cannot reasonably be denied that we have a long way to go before we create in this part of Ireland a society that would seem to be welcoming to, open to, and attractive to people of the Northern Unionist tradition.

Garret FitzGerald, the Irish Prime Minister, describing the failure of the Irish Republic to allow non-Catholics to get divorced.

SOURCE 13

Catholics pilgrims at the modern shrine to the Virgin Mary at Knock, western Ireland. The popularity of such sites shows how influential the Catholic Church is in the lives of many Catholics in Ireland.

2: POWER POLITICS

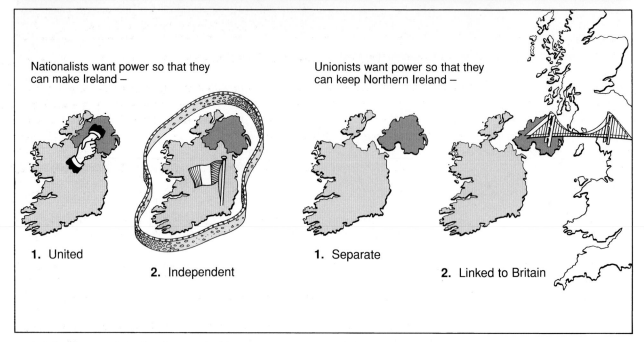

Nationalists want power so that they can make Ireland –

1. United
2. Independent

Unionists want power so that they can keep Northern Ireland –

1. Separate
2. Linked to Britain

Nationalist and Unionist traditions

Today's conflict is a struggle for power between two groups of people in Northern Ireland. This struggle is only partly about the religious differences between Catholics and Protestants. It is also a conflict about political beliefs between Nationalists and Unionists.

Nationalism

Nationalists agree that they want a united Ireland, but they disagree about the best way to get this. Some, like the SDLP, think the only way is by peaceful negotiation. This view has a long history. Others, like the IRA, have a different view. The traditional republican view is that the British will only respond to the use of violence and only the armed struggle of the IRA will achieve a united Ireland.

SOURCE 1

If the British come here to shoot our men and women, the only way is for Irish people to shoot them back. If it takes another 800 years, we'll get them out of the country. We'll come out on top because this is our country. There's only one way to send them back – that's in boxes.

Paddy Hill, one of the Birmingham Six, expressed a traditional republican view in January 1993.

In the late 1980s and early 1990s, Gerry Adams of Sinn Féin and John Hume of the SDLP met to work out a common approach. Adams agreed to work towards a peaceful approach to politics. He persuaded the IRA to change, and in 1994 and 1997 the IRA declared cease-fires. The 1997 cease-fire was followed by peace talks which were attended by both Sinn Féin and the SDLP. Both Nationalist parties agreed to support the Good Friday Agreement in 1998. Some Unionists have been disturbed by the way that Adams and Hume have worked together.

SOURCE 2

Everyone has a solemn duty to change the political climate away from conflict and towards a process of national reconciliation which sees the peaceful accommodation of the differences between the people of Britain and Ireland and the Irish people themselves. In striving for that end, we accept than an internal settlement (within Northern Ireland) is not a solution because it obviously does not deal with all the relationships at the heart of the problem.

We accept that the Irish people as a whole have a right to national self-determination. This is a view shared by a majority of the people of this island, though not by all its people. We are mindful that not all the people of Ireland agree (with us).

We see the task of reaching agreement on a peaceful and democratic accord for all on this island as our primary challenge.

A joint statement by Gerry Adams and John Hume, April 1993

❖ *Why do you think that many people were surprised to hear that John Hume and Gerry Adams were talking to each other?*

❖ *Why do you think that many Unionists were unhappy with the Hume-Adams talks?*

IRISH NATIONALISM: IDEAS AND ACTIONS

Wolfe Tone's 'address to the people of Ireland'

"Six hundred years of slavery have passed over our fathers' heads. It is England who deprives our wretched peasantry of their rights as human beings. You must choose between slavery or independence. I do not doubt your decision: liberty for yourselves and independence for your country."

Fenian oath sworn in Dublin, 1858

"I swear to renounce all allegiance to the Queen of England and to take up arms and fight to make Ireland an independent democratic republic."

Patrick Pearce. Easter Rebel and IRB leader

"We come here to complete the work of Tone. Tone has stated our programme for us to break the connection with England the never-failing source of all our evils! Ireland will not find Christ's peace till she has taken Christ's sword. We must not faint at the sight of blood."

The Easter Rebels' Proclamation of the Irish Republic, Easter 1916

"We declare the right of the people of Ireland to the ownership of Ireland. In every generation the Irish have declared their right to national freedom. Six times in the past 300 years they have asserted it in arms."

IRA manifesto 1956

"This is an age-old struggle against British aggression. It is up to this generation of Irish men and women to receive for all time our unity, independence and freedom from foreign domination."

Provisional IRA statement 1979

"The British government continue to oppress our people. Well, for this we will tear our their imperialist heart."

Danny Morrison, Sinn Féin Conference 1983

"Is there any one here who objects to taking power with a ballot paper in one hand and an Armalite rifle in the other?"

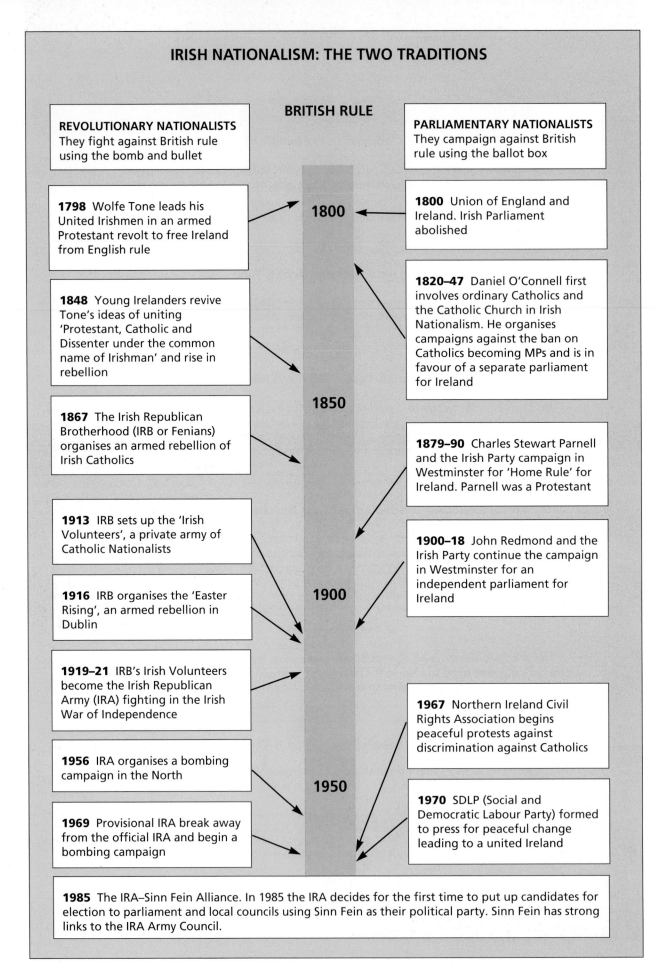

IRISH NATIONALISM: THE TWO TRADITIONS

BRITISH RULE

REVOLUTIONARY NATIONALISTS
They fight against British rule using the bomb and bullet

PARLIAMENTARY NATIONALISTS
They campaign against British rule using the ballot box

1798 Wolfe Tone leads his United Irishmen in an armed Protestant revolt to free Ireland from English rule

1800

1800 Union of England and Ireland. Irish Parliament abolished

1820–47 Daniel O'Connell first involves ordinary Catholics and the Catholic Church in Irish Nationalism. He organises campaigns against the ban on Catholics becoming MPs and is in favour of a separate parliament for Ireland

1848 Young Irelanders revive Tone's ideas of uniting 'Protestant, Catholic and Dissenter under the common name of Irishman' and rise in rebellion

1850

1867 The Irish Republican Brotherhood (IRB or Fenians) organises an armed rebellion of Irish Catholics

1879–90 Charles Stewart Parnell and the Irish Party campaign in Westminster for 'Home Rule' for Ireland. Parnell was a Protestant

1913 IRB sets up the 'Irish Volunteers', a private army of Catholic Nationalists

1900–18 John Redmond and the Irish Party continue the campaign in Westminster for an independent parliament for Ireland

1916 IRB organises the 'Easter Rising', an armed rebellion in Dublin

1900

1919–21 IRB's Irish Volunteers become the Irish Republican Army (IRA) fighting in the Irish War of Independence

1967 Northern Ireland Civil Rights Association begins peaceful protests against discrimination against Catholics

1956 IRA organises a bombing campaign in the North

1950

1970 SDLP (Social and Democratic Labour Party) formed to press for peaceful change leading to a united Ireland

1969 Provisional IRA break away from the official IRA and begin a bombing campaign

1985 The IRA–Sinn Fein Alliance. In 1985 the IRA decides for the first time to put up candidates for election to parliament and local councils using Sinn Fein as their political party. Sinn Fein has strong links to the IRA Army Council.

UNIONISM

Unionists are determined to stop North and South becoming united, but they disagree about the best way to do this. Some, like the politicians of the Ulster Unionist Party and the Democratic Unionist Party, use parliamentary politics to protect the Union with Britain. Others, including members of the UDA and the UVF, have used violence against Catholics in an attempt to defeat the IRA. The Protestant paramilitaries have carried out campaigns of sectarian murder, during which innocent Catholics have been killed as a warning to the IRA. Occasionally the line between the Parliamentary Unionists and the use of paramilitary force becomes blurred. Ian Paisley, for example, has stated that if necessary his followers would use force to resist government from Dublin. Members of both parties have repeatedly called for much tougher action by the security forces against the IRA.

SOURCE 1

You either be killed by the IRA or kill them and I want to see them dead. Something has to be done to finish this trouble once and for all and the only way to do this with the IRA is to kill them.

Gregory Campbell, Democratic Unionist Party Councillor, 1985.

SOURCE 2

Members of the UDA.

Remember 1690

Since their arrival in Ireland in the 17th century, Protestants have felt threatened by the greater number of Irish Catholics. Many modern Protestants still have a defensive and suspicious attitude to Catholics. This attitude is seen in the activities of the Orange Order.

Today 100,000 Protestants are members of the Orange Order. Most Unionist politicians over the last 100 years have also been Orangemen. Their hero is William of Orange. They believe that his victory at the Battle of the Boyne saved Protestants from destruction at the hands of their Catholic enemies. For many of them the 17th century struggle still goes on today and they relive it in different ways.

SOURCE 3

A drawing of King William of Orange from a purse of an Orangeman c.1800. On it are the words 'The immortal memory of 1690'.

SOURCE 4

To the glorious memory of King William III, who saved us from Slaves and Slavery, Knaves and Knavery, Popes and Popery. Whoever denies this toast may be crammed and jammed into the muzzle of the great gun of Athlone and fired into the Pope's belly, and the Pope into the Devil's belly and the Devil into hell, and the door locked and the key in an Orangeman's pocket.

An Orange Order toast from about 1800.

SOURCE 5

Question:
How can I help to keep Ulster Protestant, loyal and British?

Answer:
a. by being a faithful member of my own church.

b. by being a regular member of my own junior Loyal Orange Lodge.

c. by showing in my own character that the Ulster-British way of life is worth having and holding.

An extract from the Junior Orangeman's Catechism, 1966.

Remember 1912

The idea of using force to resist government from Dublin goes back to early days of the Unionist Party in the 1880s. This was the time when Parnell was campaigning for Home Rule. Protestants wanted to stop all plans for an all-Ireland Parliament based in Dublin and dominated by Catholics. So they formed the Ulster Unionist Party. Although this was a political party of Protestant MPs, they made it clear that if pushed too far 'Ulster will fight'. This has been the rallying cry of Unionist politicians and private armies ever since.

In 1912 it seemed certain that a Dublin parliament would finally be set up. So Unionists made plans to stop this by force. Led by Edward Carson, they prepared a separate government for an independent Ulster. At the same time they formed their own private army, the Ulster Volunteer Force, to defend themselves. Carson is the hero of Unionist politicians and private armies today.

Carson's action convinced the British that Ulster would have to be left out of an independent Ireland. From 1921–72 the North was ruled by a Unionist government. In these years Unionists saw the North as their country and were determined to keep it that way. Again they were prepared to use force. Catholics were seen as potential traitors and an armed Protestant police force made sure they did not get out of hand.

In the 1960s Unionist politicians began to take a more sympathetic attitude to Nationalists in the North and the South. Again ordinary Protestants began to fear the idea of a united Ireland. They began to attack Catholic civil rights marchers and 'The Troubles' began.

Since 1970, many Unionists have looked back to the days of Carson when politicians and private armies joined together to fight for Ulster. Ian Paisley set up a new hardline Democratic Unionist Party. The DUP tried to replace the Official Unionist Party as the main representative of the Protestant people. The UVF and the UDA have been formed to carry on the tradition of Carson's original Ulster Volunteer Force.

SOURCE 7

Armed B Specials at a road block in the 1930s.

SOURCE 6

Carson and the Ulster Volunteer Force, 1914.

The Unionists and the British

The Protestant people of Northern Ireland have a complex relationship with the British on the mainland. Many Protestants see themselves as being 'British'. In a survey conducted in 1989 70% of the Protestants interviewed said that they were 'British'. People in mainland Britain, particularly in England, tend to see the Protestants as being 'Irish'.

Protestants say that they are loyal to the British monarchy, or the 'Crown'. They are much less committed to the government in London. Some Unionists believe that the British government would like to see a united Ireland.

SOURCE 7

Ian Paisley paraded 500 men from a private Protestant army today. He said 'These men are ready to fight and die rather than accept an all-Ireland Republic. They are prepared to defend their province in the same way as Lord Carson and the men of the Ulster Volunteer Force!'

Report from the *London New Standard*, 6 February 1981.

SOURCE 8

Ian Paisley.

SOURCE 9

The depth of Protestant suspicions of the British government was seen in the reaction to the Anglo-Irish Agreement. Speaking in his church in Belfast, Ian Paisley called upon God to punish the British Prime Minister for her treachery to Ulster:

'We pray this night that thou wouldst deal with the Prime Minister of our country. O God, in wrath take vengeance on this wicked, treacherous lying woman. Take vengeance upon her, O Lord, and grant that we shall see a demonstration of Thy power.'

Ian Paisley, 1985.

The decline of the DUP?

In the 1970s it seemed that Ian Paisley's DUP might become the single largest party representing the Unionist people. The tide turned in the 1980s and 1990s and the Ulster Unionist Party successfully met the challenge of the DUP. The Anglo-Irish Agreement of 1985 played a part in this development. Paisley and his party obstinately opposed the Agreement and made angry speeches, but these protests achieved nothing and this reduced the credibility of the party. The Ulster Unionist Party was more moderate and seemed to be more successful in influencing the British government.

In 1995 David Trimble became the new leader of the Ulster Unionist Party. While Paisley and the DUP boycotted the peace talks in 1997 and early 1998, Trimble and the UUP played a full part in the talks. The gulf between the two Unionist parties increased as a result of the Good Friday Agreement of 1998. The UUP supported the Agreement and the new power-sharing assembly for Northern Ireland. Trimble became the First Minister of the assembly. Paisley's party denounced the settlement, and called Trimble a 'traitor'.

❖ *What is the Orange Order? What part does it play in the lives of the Protestant community?*
❖ *Why do you think that many Unionists mistrust the British government?*
❖ *Which party has been more successful in the 1990s: the Democratic Unionist Party or the Ulster Unionist Party?*

3: ECONOMICS

The land question

In the 17th century the British government decided that in order to stop rebellions in Ireland they would have to put loyal subjects in control of the land of Ireland. The government started taking land from the native Irish (who were Catholic rebels) and giving it to Scottish and English settlers (who were loyal Protestants). The first stage in this massive transfer of land was the 'Plantation' of Ulster in 1609. In 1607 the two main landowners in the province, the Earls of Tyrone and Tyrconnell, fled to France after they were caught up in a rebellion plot with Spain. Their lands were seized and sold off to wealthy English and Scottish landowners or merchants. They, in turn, let out their new land to English and Scottish tenants or to Irish tenants willing to pay much higher rents. Many poor Irish tenants were forced to take barren, hilly areas that the settlers did not want. Others were reduced to working as labourers for the newcomers.

After the rebellions in 1641 and 1690 more land was confiscated from Catholic landowners and settled in the same way. Finally in 1704 the Irish Parliament (which was controlled by Protestant landowners) passed a law forbidding Catholics to buy any more land. By 1703 over 80% of the land was owned by Protestants – though Ulster was the only province with large numbers of settlers.

Although the Protestants took control of the countryside in the 17th and 18th centuries there was a continuing tradition of violent resistance on the part of Catholic labourers. Cattle belonging to the landlords were often maimed. In the 18th century rebellious Catholics organised themselves into secret gangs, with names like 'the Defenders' and 'the Ribbonmen'.

Tenant and landlord

By the beginning of the 19th century, arguments about land began to dominate Irish politics. Catholics deeply resented the loss of their lands and the harsh treatment they often received from Protestant landlords. When Daniel O'Connell and the Parliamentary Nationalists looked for support, they soon attracted the backing of discontented Catholics in the countryside. Many farms were divided and had become very small. Some landlords evicted tenants to make bigger holdings. This caused even more bitterness among Catholics.

SOURCE 1

Control of the land gave Protestant landlords extraordinary power over their Catholic tenants. Arthur Young, an English visitor in 1776, was amazed at the way poor Catholics were violently treated by their landlords.

A landlord in Ireland can scarcely invent an order which a servant, labourer or cottar dares to refuse to execute. Nothing satisfies him but an unlimited submission. Disrespect he may punish with his cane or his horsewhip. A poor man would have his bones broke if he offered to lift his hand in his own defence. Landlords have assured me that many of their cottars would think themselves honoured by having their wives and daughters sent for to the bed of their masters.

SOURCE 2

A 19th-century cartoon of peasants being crushed by a cruel landlord.

After the Famine many Protestant landlords evicted the Catholic tenants to increase the value of the land.

The Great Famine and the Land War

Catholic resentment of their treatment by Protestant landlords was greatly increased by the Great Famine of 1845–49. About a million Irish people died of starvation and more emigrated. Evictions continued after the Famine, and so did the anger of the Catholics of the countryside.

In 1879 a Fenian revolutionary, Michael Davitt, founded the Land League. Between 1879 and 1882 the Land League organised a campaign of intimidation and violence in the Irish countryside to win a better deal for poor tenant farmers.

Unrest brings land reforms

In the late 19th century British politicians decided that reforms were needed in the Irish countryside, in order to stop the unrest. Between 1870 and 1903 various laws were passed that gave greater protection to tenants, and helped many thousands of them to buy their farms from their Protestant landlords. By the outbreak of the First World War, Catholics had won back control of much of the land taken from their ancestors in the 17th century. In 1870 they had owned 3% of the land; by 1916 this figure had risen to 64%.

Economics, Unionists and Partition 1880–1920

In the 1790s the economic grievances had led a few Protestants to demand Irish independence. By the end of the 19th century most Ulster Protestants no longer wanted Ireland to become independent of Britain. In the 1880s they set up the Ulster Unionist Party to fight to keep Ireland's links with Britain. It was the fierce opposition of Unionist politicians and private armies in 1912–14 which made the British government decide that Ireland would have to be divided into two.

SOURCE 3

The landlords do not now and never did belong to this island. Tyrants they have been since first they set foot on our soil. I say that the soil of a country belongs to the people of that country, no to any one class.

An early Nationalist looks for support: Fintan Lalor, *The Irish Felon*, 1848.

SOURCE 4

As part of the UK we have shared in the progress of industry in the great centres of England. How would our commercial interests be represented in a parliament in Dublin? We all know Ireland is an agricultural country. We are not prepared to come under the rule of a Dublin parliament dominated by poor farmers.

Belfast factory owners oppose Home Rule, 1893.

❖ *How have arguments about land encouraged Irish Catholics to be hostile towards Britain?*

❖ *How did economics encourage Protestants to become Unionists in the 19th century?*

ECONOMICS AND DIVISIONS IN THE NORTH 1920–72

During the years 1921–72 Northern Ireland was ruled by the Ulster Unionist Party as a separate state within the United Kingdom. Throughout this time economics continued to divide the two communities. The creation of the new state of Northern Ireland coincided with the decline of Ulster's traditional industries: shipbuilding and linen. Northern Ireland was badly hit by the Depression that swept the world in the 1930s. The result was a high level of unemployment in both communities. However, unemployment for men was consistently worse in Catholic areas. After the Second World War there was some economic recovery but unemployment remained a problem in some Catholic areas.

The Unionist government of Northern Ireland was not active in social matters and did very little to improve living conditions for ordinary people. In some ways living standards deteriorated under Stormont rule. In contrast with the rest of the UK, the rate of death among mothers in childbirth increased by 20% in 1922–38.

If Northern Ireland had been a very prosperous place, some of the hostility between Catholic and Protestant might gradually have disappeared. The problems of poverty ensured that this did not happen. These problems were made worse by the deliberate discrimination practised against Catholics by powerful Unionists. Between 1925 and 1949 not a single Catholic was appointed as a judge to the Supreme Court. A survey in 1943 showed that of the 55 most senior civil servants in Northern Ireland not one was a Catholic. Discrimination also applied to housing. Catholics were much less likely to be given decent council houses. The town of Dungannon was evenly divided among Catholics and Protestants. Protestants ran the local council and for over thirty years not a single Catholic was given a permanent council house.

SOURCE 1

Many of you employ Catholics but I have not one about the house. In Northern Ireland the Catholic population is increasing. 97% of Catholics in Ireland are disloyal and disruptive. If we allow Catholics to work on our farms we are traitors to Ulster.

Basil Brooke, Minister of Agriculture in Northern Ireland, 12 July 1933.

SOURCE 2

Most of my life I have been brought up as a Nationalist. However I grew up in a situation of such degradation and unemployment that the life our people lived was no life at all. I said to myself—when I grow up and get married I will want something better for my children than this.

A republican quoted by Sean Cronin, *Irish Nationalism*, 1980.

SOURCE 4

'One house, one man, one job': the economic demands of the Civil Rights marchers, 1968.

SOURCE 3

Catholic slums, 1955.

Economics and today's conflict

Northern Ireland remains one of the poorest and most deprived parts of the United Kingdom. During the 20th century the greatest poverty and unemployment has been experienced by the Catholic/Nationalist people. Today the greatest support for the IRA is in the poor urban ghettos in Derry and Belfast. Undoubtedly poverty has encouraged some people to turn towards the IRA.

Since the British government began direct rule in 1972 it has tried to stop employers discriminating against Catholics. In 1976 it set up the Fair Employment Agency to check up on any discrimination. In 1989 the government abolished the Fair Employment Agency and replaced it with a new organisation called the Fair Employment Commission. The government was not satisfied with progress under the Fair Employment Agency and wanted to replace it with a new body with more power to tackle discrimination. Yet, after thirteen years of anti-discrimination laws, male Catholic unemployment remained twice as high as male Protestant unemployment.

Today Catholic men are still much more likely to be unemployed. The work of the Fair Employment Commission has been undermined by an overall rise in unemployment. In 1968 there 40,000 unemployed people in Northern Ireland. Today the figure is about 100,000. Catholics are still over-represented in some unskilled jobs and still under-represented in some managerial posts. In the early 1990s Queen's University, Belfast, for example, had 65% Catholic students. However, fewer than 10% of the lecturers were Catholic. There has been some progress in fair employment, however, particularly in the civil service. In 1973 only 5% of senior civil servants in Northern Ireland were Catholic. By the mid-1990s the figure had risen to 20%. But this is still less than the proportion of Catholics in the overall population (about 33%).

SOURCE 5

One of the strongholds of IRA/Sinn Féin support is West Belfast. This area has had longstanding economic problems.

Many parts of West Belfast have always been one huge poverty trap. The area has the worst unemployment, the worst housing, the worst health of any place in Northern Ireland. It holds around 90,000 people. The jobless figure for the Whiterock ward is 56%. West Belfast is a huge ghetto, almost totally Catholic, bounded by mountains, swamp, a motorway, and hostile loyalist districts.

David McKittrick, The *Independent*, 1988

SOURCE 6

Unemployment often led young people to involvement in political violence. In May 1992 a British journalist interviewed unemployed Protestant youths in Belfast.

In his spare time Stuart sniffs glue. He nicks about two cars a week to go joyriding. He beats up and throws petrol bombs at Catholics, 'because its a good laugh fighting people you don't like'.

The *Guardian*, 1992

❖ *In what ways were Catholics discriminated against in the period 1920–72?*
❖ *Why are some Catholics unhappy at the way jobs are distributed in modern Northern Ireland?*

SOURCE 7

The bleak streets of West Belfast.

4: SOCIAL LIFE

As well as political, religious and economic causes there are also social causes of today's conflict in Ireland. These are connected with the way people carry on their everyday lives at home and at school.

Separate schools

Today, the two communities are not only divided by religion and politics, they also go to separate schools.

Like other causes of the conflict, the idea of separate schools has a long history. In 1700 after their victory at the Battle of the Boyne, Protestants passed a series of 'Penal Laws' against Catholics. One of these banned Catholic teachers and carried a penalty of life imprisonment for those who broke this law.

For over 100 years the only legal schools were those run by the Protestant churches. Catholics ran illegal 'hedge' schools for their children. Then, in 1831, the British government provided money to pay for schools for both groups. The government wanted these schools to have both Catholic and Protestant pupils, but the churchmen on both sides insisted on separate schools. When Northern Ireland was set up in the 1920s another attempt was made to have 'mixed' religion schools for all children. Again this was wrecked by churchmen on both sides.

◆ *Look at the following sources. How do they help us to understand how education has contributed to the conflict in Ireland?*

SOURCE 1

Only Catholics played Gaelic games, like this contest of hurley.

SOURCE 2

Our schools drummed into us the Protestant story. On leaving school I had no notion of the past other than a few dreary details about our Protestant faith, the darkness of Rome, and for comic relief, intimate details of the Popes' private lives. We knew nothing of the Catholic world. That Catholics were allowed to live in London with our Protestant King seemed impossible.

A Protestant education in the 1930s: adapted from R. Harbinson, *No Surrender*, 1961.

SOURCE 3

The teachers liked to pretend it was a civilised outpost of England: rugby, cricket and English headmasters. There was little to suggest we were living in Ireland – no Irish history, no Irish literature, no Irish music. I could rhyme off the names of English kings and queens but hardly even heard of Wolfe Tone and Daniel O'Connell.

A Protestant grammar school in the 1950s: N. Longley, *New Statesman*, 1974.

SOURCE 4

St Patrick's Academy Dungannon, where I went, was a patriotic school. It owed its proudly Irish slant to the Vice-Principal, Mother Benignus. She disliked the English. All her family had suffered at the hands of the British forces. She was very keen about Irish culture which drives lots of people away who couldn't take it for breakfast, dinner and tea. She didn't hate Protestants. But her view was that you couldn't very well put up with them, they weren't Irish.

We learned Irish history. The interpretations we were given were very different from Protestant history books.

A Catholic grammar school in the 1960s: Bernadette Devlin, *The Price of My Soul*, 1969.

Separate housing

In the cities of Belfast and Derry, most Catholics and Protestants live in separate areas. In Derry this goes back to the time of the Protestant Plantations in the early 17th century. Derry was given to a Company of London merchants. They rebuilt and fortified the town, renaming it Londonderry. Catholics had to live outside the walls 'by the bogside'. Today Derry's Bogside district is a stronghold of Nationalism.

Separate areas in Belfast grew up in the early 19th century when the growing shipbuilding and linen industries attracted many Catholic workers. Catholic migrants moved into the Falls Road area. Many Protestant workers lived in the nearby Shankill Road area. The first riots between Catholics and Protestants in Belfast began in 1832. Others have followed at intervals up to the present day. In the early days of the current crisis many people who lived in the 'wrong' area – that is Catholics in Protestant areas and vice versa – were forced to leave their homes.

SOURCE 5

Derry in 1686. The area within the walls was for Protestants; Catholics had to live outside.

SOURCE 6

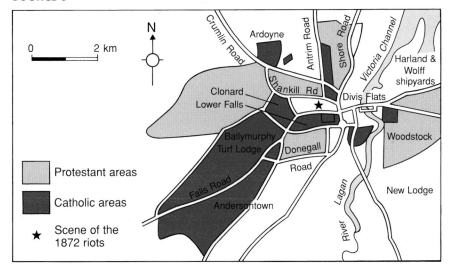

SOURCE 7

The two sides met for a battle in the brick fields between the Shankill and Falls Road. The police tried in vain to separate them and the military were sent for. The houses on the Shankill Road have been gutted by mobs. Protestants living in Catholic areas and Catholics living in Protestant districts have found it necessary to change their quarters.

Illustrated London News, 15 August 1872.

SOURCE 8

As he turned into his street he felt the eyes on him. He could not bear to look up and see the flutter of the Union Jacks and the Ulster flag. Of late there were more and more of these appearing in the estate. It was a dangerous sign that the Loyalists were getting angry. The flags should all have been down now because 12th July was long past.

Even looking at his feet Cal couldn't avoid the repulsion because the kerbstones had been painted red, white and blue. Cal felt that it was aimed at them, the McCluskeys, because his father and he were the only Catholic family left in the whole estate. Fear had driven the others out but his father would not move. 'No Loyalist bastard is going to drive me out of my home. They can kill me first'.

From *Cal*, a novel by Bernard MacLaverty, 1983.

The tendency for Catholics and Protestants to live apart has increased since 1968. The 1991 census showed that more than half of the population lived in areas that were either solidly Protestant or solidly Catholic. The segregation was most marked among poorer, working-class people in the cities of Belfast and Derry. Some attempts have been made in recent years to encourage mixed schools of Catholics and Protestants but by the 1990s these educated only a tiny fraction of the overall population of Northern Ireland.

❖ *Why do you think working-class Catholics and Protestants tend to live apart?*

❖ *How has separate housing contributed to the modern conflict?*

The Catholic and Protestant ghettoes of Belfast.

1: THE TRIUMPH OF SINN FÉIN 1918

From 1798 to 1914 the Revolutionary Nationalists had looked like losers (page 16). Their rebellions had been crushed and ordinary Catholics had refused to support their aims or their methods. By 1914 most Catholics supported the political leaders of the Irish Nationalist Party and their peaceful campaign for an Irish parliament.

John Redmond, leader of the parliamentary Irish Party, speaking to a crowd in Dublin, 1912

By 1918 all this had changed. In the general election of that year the majority of Irish Catholics voted for Sinn Féin, the Revolutionary Nationalist Party. Sinn Féin now had 73 MPs and the Irish Nationalist Party just six MPs. The Revolutionaries had triumphed at last. This shift in public opinion made a big difference to the future of Ireland.

Why did Revolutionary Nationalists enjoy an upsurge in support?

Historians have suggested several possible causes:

- The 'Irish Ireland' movement.
- Unionist opposition to Home Rule.
- Irish Nationalist Party involvement in the First World War.
- The 1916 Easter Rising.
- The conscription crisis of 1918.

Look at the information on pages 60–63. Explain in your own words how each factor contributed to the rise of Revolutionary Nationalism.

Which factor do you think was the most important cause of the Sinn Féin triumph in 1918?

A The 'Irish Ireland' Movement

In the late 19th century many people became interested in Ireland's Gaelic past. They felt that Ireland was getting too much like England, and that the Irish language and Irish games should be used in place of ideas imported from Britain. The call for a more 'Irish Ireland' led to the development of new political ideas. Some questioned the need for any sort of link between Ireland and Britain.

In 1905 a Dublin journalist, Arthur Griffith, founded a political party called 'Sinn Féin' (which means in Gaelic 'Ourselves Alone'). Griffith wanted all Irish MPs to leave the House of Commons and set up an independent Irish parliament in Dublin.

◆ *Look at the following sources. How important was the Irish Ireland movement politically?*

SOURCE 1

An Irish book produced in 1922. How can you tell that the artist was interested in Ireland's Gaelic past?

SOURCE 2

All this had little political impact. Neither Irish speakers nor hurley players not even poets were going to break the connection with England.

J. Bowyer Bell, *The Secret Army*, 1970.

Sinn Féin attracted many young republicans, and people who were disappointed with Home Rule. In 1908 Sinn Féin fought a by-election against a Home Ruler. The party was defeated and declined after that but Griffith did not give up hope.

M. E. Collins, 1972.

B   Ulster Unionist opposition to Home Rule

The aim of the Parliamentary Nationalists was to win Home Rule. This meant a separate parliament for the whole of Ireland based in Dublin and controlled by the Catholic majority.

In 1912 the Liberal Prime Minister, Asquith, brought in the Third Home Rule Bill which was due to become law in 1914. The Irish Party leader, John Redmond, was delighted with the progress of Home Rule in 1912. His party seemed to have finally achieved its aim. Unfortunately for Redmond the Ulster Unionists, led by Edward Carson, declared that they would fight rather than accept Home Rule. The Ulster Volunteer Force was set up to back up this threat.

By 1914 Redmond had reluctantly agreed that Ulster should be allowed to opt out of a Dublin parliament. When the First World War broke out in August 1914 the British declared that a final decision on Irish independence would have to wait until the end of the war.

How do you think this Unionist opposition affected support for Redmond and the Irish party after the war?

C   The Irish Party and the War

There were two private armies in Ireland in 1914. Nationalists formed the Irish Volunteers as a counter to the Ulster Volunteer Force. The Irish Volunteers were a mixture of Parliamentary and Revolutionary Nationalists. When the First World War began John Redmond urged Volunteers to join the British army. 80,000 Catholic Volunteers served with the British army – many of them died in the trenches in France.

SOURCE 4

The English have got all they wanted from Ireland and don't care two pence about her feelings. The people are full of indignation but are powerless. It almost makes me cry to think of Irish soldiers fighting not for Ireland but for Carson and what he stands for. Home Rule is dead and buried and the Irish Party is a tool of the British Empire. What the future holds in store for us God knows. There is a great revulsion of feeling in Ireland.

From a letter by the Catholic Bishop of Killaloe, June 1915. The Bishop had previously supported the Irish Party.

SOURCE 5

In May 1915 Asquith formed a coalition government bringing together Liberals and Conservatives and including Carson as Attorney General. The inclusion of the Ulster Unionist leader in the government was a blow to Redmond and the Nationalists – almost a slap in the face. The heart went out of the Irish Party.

C. L. Mowat, *The Irish Question in British Politics*, 1966.

SOURCE 6

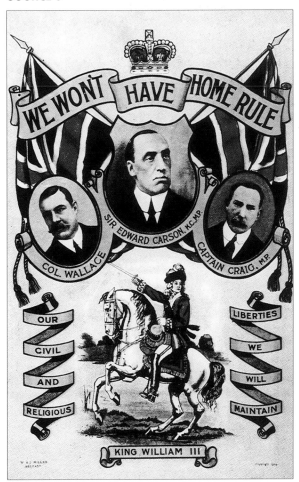

A Unionist poster backing Carson's opposition to Home Rule.

D The Easter Rising 1916

A Fenian group, the Irish Republican Brotherhood, decided that the war was a good opportunity to stage an armed uprising against the British. Their leader, Patrick Pearse, had been deeply influenced by the Irish Ireland movement and he despised the Irish Party. When Redmond showed his support for the British war effort, the revolutionary Nationalists left the Irish Volunteers and set up their own rival force. Pearse planned to use these men in a rebellion.

The rising started on Easter Monday 1916 when the rebels seized control of the centre of Dublin. From the steps of the General Post Office, Pearse declared that the rebels were 'the provisional government of the Irish Republic'. The British forces soon surrounded the rebels who were hopelessly outnumbered. After six days of fighting Pearse surrendered. The British army, under General Maxwell, executed fifteen of the leaders.

SOURCE 7

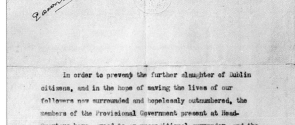

The rebels' surrender note, signed by Patrick Pearse.

SOURCE 8

The executions of the rebel leaders in Kilmainham Jail, Dublin, 1916.

Sinn Féin had not been involved in the organisation of the Easter Rising but afterwards it gained many new recruits. Survivors of the rebellion, such as Eamon de Valera, added new strength to the party. Throughout 1917 Sinn Féin grew more powerful. For the first time it defeated Irish Party candidates in several by-elections.

SOURCE 9

You are washing out our whole life's work in a sea of blood. Thousands of people in Dublin, who ten days ago were bitterly opposed to the whole of the Sinn Féin movement and to the rebellion, are now becoming infuriated against the government on account of these executions.

An Irish Party MP criticises British policy after the Easter Rising: John Dillon speaking to the House of Commons, 11 May 1916.

SOURCE 10

In 1916 I was in Mesopotamia [Iraq] with the British Expeditionary Force. Outside the orderly room I saw a notice. It told us of this rising in Dublin, and the executions of men I'd never heard of – I said to myself, 'What the hell am I doing with the British army? It's with the Irish I should be'

Tom Barry, later a commander of the IRA, speaking in 'Curious Journey', 1982.

SOURCE 11

The newspapers and the public called it the 'Sinn Féin' rebellion. Although Sinn Féin had had nothing to do with it, so little was known of the Rising's real leaders and their motives that a link with Sinn Féin seemed the only explanation.

Robert Kee, *Ireland – A History*, 1980.

E Conscription, 1918

By March 1918, the British were running short of men in the war with Germany. The government decided to bring in conscription in Ireland: this meant that Irish men would be forced to join the British Army.

SOURCE 12

No one who had not been in Ireland during the past six weeks can possibly realise how passionate is the resentment which has been aroused by conscription. Men are ready to take to the hills or die fighting in their homes rather than be compelled to join the Army. The tension is extraordinary.

Hugh Law, an Irish Party MP, June 1918.

SOURCE 13

The only recent result of conscription had been to give a tremendous fillip to Sinn Féin, so that during the year the number of members grew from 66,270 to 120,00. The conscription threat was, indeed, second only to the execution of the Easter week leaders in creating a substantial backing for Sinn Féin among the Irish people.

Edgar Holt, *Protest in Arms*, 1960

SOURCE 14

The anti-conscription oath of 1918 won the backing of the Catholic Church, as this document shows.

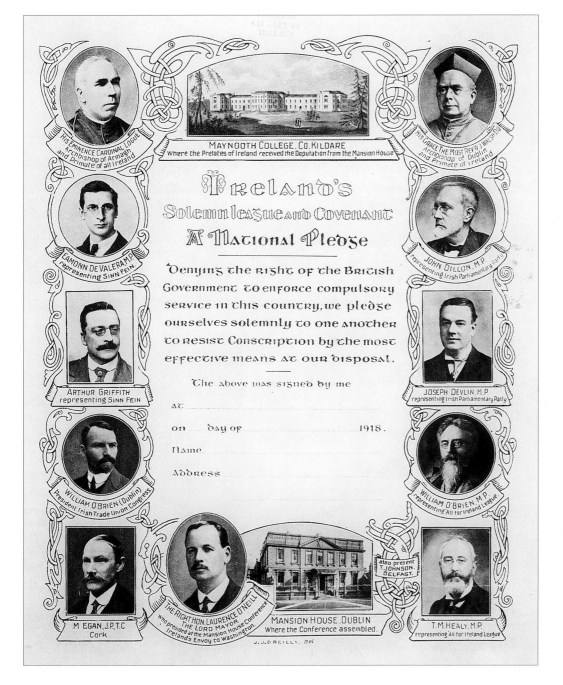

2: DIVIDING IRELAND 1920 – 21

The Irish War of Independence

After the 1918 election most Irish MPs were members of Sinn Féin, and they wanted a complete break with Britain. In January 1919 these MPs set up their own parliament in Dublin, the Dáil Éireann. This declared itself the government of an independent Irish Republic. Soon after, the survivors of the Easter Rising were reorganised as the Irish Republican Army (IRA).

The Black and Tans

For most of 1919 there was an uneasy peace. Then in 1920 the IRA began a guerrilla war against the Royal Irish Constabulary. The RIC were armed and still controlled by the British. The IRA staged surprise attacks on police stations and patrols. Suspected police informers were shot.

The British sent the RIC reinforcements. These recruits were called the 'Black and Tans' because of the colours of their makeshift uniforms. The Black and Tans soon won a reputation for great brutality. IRA suspects were beaten and sometimes killed. After an IRA attack the Black and Tans often burned down the houses of local Catholics.

Ulster goes it alone

By 1920 British rule in Ireland was collapsing. The only part not controlled by Sinn Féin and the IRA was Ulster. Here the Protestant private army, the Ulster Volunteer Force (UVF), was ready to fight to keep the North out of an independent Ireland. The British Government tried to end the crisis by dividing the six most Protestant counties of Ulster from the rest of Ireland. The two parts, Northern and Southern Ireland, were to stay part of the United Kingdom but they were also to be given their own local parliaments.

The Northern Unionists reluctantly accepted the new arrangements. Sinn Féin rejected them. The guerrilla war continued.

SOURCE 1

The Dáil Éirean in 1921, with de Valera acting as chairman.

The peace talks

By the summer of 1921 there was a stalemate in the war. Neither side was close to victory. In July 1921 a truce was arranged. Sinn Féin leaders were invited to London to talk about a peace treaty between the Nationalists and the British. Between July and December 1921 three groups were involved in tense negotiations about the future of Ireland: the British, the Nationalists and the Ulster Unionists.

The British government – decision makers

David Lloyd George

Lloyd George had been Prime Minister since 1916. He had few fixed views on Ireland but he wanted to be known as the man who solved the Irish problem. Whatever the solution, he had to make sure that Ireland was no longer a threat to Britain's security as she had been in the First World War (1914–18). Lloyd George was a Liberal and one of the most gifted politicians of the time. During the negotiations Lloyd George came up with an ingenious proposal: if the Unionists and Nationalists accepted partition as a temporary solution, a Boundary Commission would be set up later to decide if the boundary between North and South was fair.

Bonar Law and Austen Chamberlain

These were leaders of the Conservative Party. They had been friends and allies of Edward Carson, the Unionist leader who stood against 'Home Rule' in 1912. They were determined to protect the Ulster Unionists and keep Ireland in the British Empire.

Factors influencing their decision

SOURCE 3

Lloyd George's was a coalition government. Some of the Conservative members were opposed to Irish Independence and had very close links with Ulster Unionists. On balance, it does seem that Lloyd George really was anxious to settle the Irish problem by setting up an All-Ireland Parliament in Dublin. He took as hard a line with Craig as he dared, but he had sworn not to force Ulster into a united Ireland and he did not want civil war. Neither did he want divisions in his Cabinet.

Carlton Younger, *A State of Disunion*, 1972.

SOURCE 4

Sinn Féin rules the country – and rules it admirably. Crimes of any kind are dealt with the Sinn Féin courts, who try the accused with perfect fairness. Missing property, if reported to the Sinn Féin police, is inevitably found and restored to the owners.

Letter from a Limerick landlord, 1920.

SOURCE 5

Lloyd George had just been warned that Ireland could be reconquered only by a full-scale war and an army of 100,000 men.

A. J. P. Taylor, *English History 1914–1945*, 1965.

SOURCE 2

THE KINDEST CUT OF ALL.

Welsh Wizard. "I NOW PROCEED TO CUT THIS MAP INTO TWO PARTS AND PLACE THEM IN THE HAT. AFTER A SUITABLE INTERVAL THEY WILL BE FOUND TO HAVE COME TOGETHER OF THEIR OWN ACCORD—(ASIDE)—AT LEAST LET'S HOPE SO; I'VE NEVER DONE THIS TRICK BEFORE."

'The kindest cut of all'. Newspaper cartoon showing Lloyd George as a magician cutting up Ireland.

Irish Nationalists – decision makers

Eamon de Valera

Since 1919 de Valera had been the President of the Dáil government. He was anxious for peace, but he was also determined to see an Irish Republic which included Ulster. He did not go to the negotiations in London but kept in close touch.

Arthur Griffith

Griffith was the founder of Sinn Féin and the leader of the Irish delegation to London. He hated violence and was more ready than de Valera to make a deal in order to stop the killing. His delegation were given authority to sign a treaty with the British on behalf of the Dáil.

Factors influencing their decisions

SOURCE 6

IRA estimates of armed men on both sides, 1920–21

IRA men on active service		5,000
IRA men in reserve		10,000
	total	15,000
British troops and police		65,000
Ulster Volunteer Force		20,000
B Specials		16,000
	total	101,000

SOURCE 7

In the interval between the truce and the start of negotiations, the military situation had disintegrated for the Irish. Now that dangers were over recruits flocked in for the IRA. These sunshine soldiers used their position to bully, loot and extort money. The old tight organisation had broken up. Whatever the ideas of the gunmen, the war would not be restarted. The mass of the people were content with the peace, and would give little help to the IRA. All the advantages would lie with the British forces, rested but not disbanded by the truce.

C. L. Mowat, *Britain Between the Wars*, 1956.

Soldiers inspecting a bridge blown up by the IRA.

SOURCE 8

Wisely or foolishly the Irish believed that the Boundary Commission must bring them two more counties and that the North would be made too small to carry on as a result.

Frank Pakenham, *The Treaty Negotiations*, 1966

SOURCE 9

Lloyd George was one of the most brilliant political manipulators of all time. Only de Valera at the head of the Irish delegation might have been a match for Lloyd George. Ireland's best player was kept among the reserves.

Robert Kee, *The Green Flag*, 1972

The Ulster Unionists – decision makers

James Craig

In 1921 James Craig replaced Edward Carson as the leader of the Ulster Unionists. Like Carson, Craig had been involved in the Ulster Volunteer Force (UVF) before the First World War. Originally Craig had wanted to keep the whole of Ireland as part of the United Kingdom. In May 1921, however, Craig became the first Prime Minister of Northern Ireland. Although he did not go to the negotiations, the British were in constant contact with Craig. He had many friends in the Conservative Party.

Factors influencing decisions

SOURCE 10

During the negotiations Lloyd George wrote several letters to Sir James Craig proposing Irish unity, and guaranteeing the safety of the Unionists. But the attitude of the Government of Northern Ireland was, 'What we have we hold.'

Maureen Wall, *Partition – The Ulster Question*, 1966.

Members of the Unionists' B Special armed police.

SOURCE 11

If you are unable to protect us from the machinations of Sinn Féin, we will take the matter into our own hands. We will reorganise the Ulster Volunteers. These are not mere words.

Carson's 'Battle of the Boyne' speech, 12 July 1920.

SOURCE 12

Craig met Lloyd George on December 9th and told him that the Six Counties Government would give up none of their territory. The British Prime Minister reassured him on the boundary question. It was merely a matter of tidying up.

Carlton Younger, *A State of Disunion*, 1972.

❖ *Explain in your own words how the decision was taken to divide Ireland. In your answer you should mention how:*
● *The British government lost control of much of Ireland due to IRA/Sinn Féin activities*
● *De Valera made a mistake in not being personally present at the treaty negotiations.*
● *Lloyd George used the promise of a future Boundary Commission as a way of keeping both sides happy*
● *The Unionists refused to compromise and threatened war.*

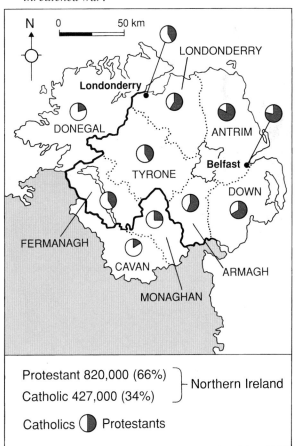

Catholics and Protestants in the nine counties of Ulster, 1911

3: THE NORTH EXPLODES 1968

The present crisis in Northern Ireland began in 1968. Since then thousands have been killed or injured. At the time, the outbreak of violence was unexpected. When Terence O'Neill took control of the government of Ulster in 1963, it seemed that Catholics and Protestants were starting to bury their old differences. O'Neill promised changes for the Catholic minority. This pleased them but his reforms were slow in coming. So in 1967 a group of Catholics started the Civil Rights Movement. A year later they organised a series of marches and demonstrations in the hope of speeding up the reforms. It was during these marches that fighting first broke out between Catholics, Protestants and the police.

Looking for a simple explanation

Here are two possible interpretations of why trouble broke out in 1968:

Explanation 1 The violence was all the fault of the IRA.

Explanation 2 The violence was the result of several causes.

Look carefully at the following evidence. Which interpretation does it support?

SOURCE 2

In 1967 we called a meeting of local leadership throughout the country to assess the strength of the movement. We discovered we had no movement.

A later republican view of the state of the IRA in 1967: Cathal Goulding, IRA leader.

SOURCE 3

The timetable of IRA involvement

1962 IRA abandons its campaign of violence because of lack of Catholic support.

1963 O'Neill promises a fairer deal for Catholics.

1967 Civil Rights movement starts.

1968 October – fighting breaks out during a march in Derry.

1969 January – fighting breaks out on a march at Burntollet Bridge

      August – more fighting between Protestants and Catholics in Belfast. The British army moves in.

      December – IRA cannot agree what action to take. It splits into groups: Official and Provisional.

1970 Provisionals begin bombing campaign.

1971 Provisionals begin to shoot British soldiers.

SOURCE 1

'What are you waiting for? All you have to do is ignore the other and go for the feller in the trench coat', newspaper cartoon.

SOURCE 4

The police view that they had on their hands an armed uprising led by the IRA was incorrect. There is no credible evidence that the IRA planned or organised the disturbances.

An official British view of early IRA involvement. From 'Report of Tribunal of Inquiry' by Justice Scarman for the British government, April 1972.

SOURCE 5

The British welfare state (developed after the war) increased family allowances and gave us a Health Service. These helped to shield Catholics from the worst effects of unemployment and poverty. Since such benefits were not available in the South, the idea of a united Ireland as the only way to make things better began to weaken.

The Education Act of 1944 gave Catholic working-class children the chance to go to grammar school and university. By the early 1960s we could easily get a place at a university but couldn't get a job as a lavatory cleaner at Derry Guildhall. That made us angry.

Eamonn McCann, 1974. McCann was a leading member of the Civil Rights movement.

SOURCE 6

Many Protestants were horrified when O'Neill visited Catholic schools.

SOURCE 7

Catholic Civil Rights marchers.

SOURCE 8

Why did the tinder which had lain around in a combustible state for so many years catch fire at this particular moment? The answer lies partly in the situation itself, but also in the rest of the world in 1968. 1968 was the year of the students' revolt. At French universities in May students brought France to a standstill.

James Callaghan, *A House Divided*, 1973. Callaghan was the British minister responsible for Northern Ireland.

SOURCE 9

In 1966 a meeting was held to discuss a Civil Rights movement for Northern Ireland like the one second-class black citizens of the United States had organised to demand their rights under the leadership of Martin Luther King.

A modern historian, Robert Kee, sees links with events in the USA.

SOURCE 10

Our route was blocked by a cordon of police about three hundred yards from the starting point. We marched into the police cordon but failed to force a way through. We noticed another police cordon had cut us off from behind. There were no exits we were trapped. The crown milled round for a few minutes, no one knowing what to do.

The two police cordons moved simultaneously onto the crowd. Men, women and children were clubbed to the ground. about a hundred had to go to hospital for treatment.

A civil rights leader later explained how violence broke out on a march in Derry, 5 October 1968.

SOURCE 11

The area was peaceful and deserted at 2 a.m. when a mob of policemen came from the city centre shouting and singing:

'Hey, hey we're the monkees,
And we're still going to monkey around,
till we see your blood flowing,
All along the ground.'

They broke in windows with their batons, kicked doors and shouted to the people to 'come out and fight, you Fenian bastards'.

McCann, the civil rights activist, describes a police visit to a Catholic area, January 1969.

SOURCE 12

Protestant police attack Catholic civil rights marchers, Derry, October 1968.

SOURCE 13

Then we came to Burntollet Bridge. From the lanes at each side of the road burst hordes of screaming people wielding bottles, iron bars, cudgels studded with nails. They waded into the march beating the hell out of everybody.

I saw a young fellow getting a thrashing from four or five of Ian Paisley's supporters with a policeman looking on. I went rampaging up the road saying not one policemen at Burntollet Bridge would live to be sorry for what he had done.

Bernadette Devlin, *The Price of my Soul*, 1969. Devlin was a leading member of the Civil Rights movement.

SOURCE 14

Catholics man the barricades in the Battle of the Bogside, Derry, August 1969.

SOURCE 15

The O'Neillites were forsaking the past, letting Ulster's enemies take a hold on the country.

A follower of Paisley, speaking in 1984.

SOURCE 16

Neither the IRA nor any Protestant organisation planned the riots. They arose from a complex political, social and economic situation. The events of 1968-9 convinced many Protestants that Catholics were trying to end the links between Northern Ireland and the United Kingdom. The same events made Catholics believe that the police were their enemy. There were six occasions during these riots when the police were seriously at fault.

Adapted from the 'Report of the Tribunal of Inquiry' by Justice Scarman, 1972.

4: THE FALL OF STORMONT

Between 1921 and 1971 the real power in Northern Ireland lay with the Stormont government in Belfast. All this came to an end on 24 March 1972 when the British government suspended the Stormont parliament and began to rule Ulster direct from London. This marked the end of 50 years of Protestant control.

One explanation for the end of Stormont is that the local Protestant politicians could not stop the violence growing after 1968. The Stormont government tried to end the crisis in three ways:

1. They brought in reforms to make Northern Ireland fairer for Catholics.

2. They arrested hundreds of suspected terrorists and locked them up without trial. This was called internment.

3. They used British soldiers to stop disorder on the streets.

None of these solutions worked. The Provisional IRA grew in strength and their campaign of bombing and shootings caused more and more casualties. Loyalist groups started to seek out and kill Catholic Nationalists. Eventually the British government decided that Stormont could no longer cope with the escalating violence and direct rule was introduced.

Look at the following information. Work out why each of the three solutions tried by the Unionist Stormont government fail?

Solution 1 : Reforms

Even before the arrival of the British army, the Stormont government had started to bring in reforms to meet the demands of Catholics. More followed. Look at the chart below:

Catholic Complaints and Unionist Reforms 1969–71

Long-standing Catholic criticisms

1. The armed B Specials were manned entirely by Protestants

2. People could be locked up without trial and mistreated in other ways under the Special Powers Act.

3. Catholics found it more difficult than Protestants to get a vote in local elections.

4. Council boundaries were fixed or 'gerrymandered' to give Unionist candidates a better chance of winning.

5. Catholics were unable to share in government power.

6. Protestants found it easier to get good council houses.

Paisley's followers called for the resignation of O'Neill

Response of the Ulster Unionist Government 1969–71

1. The B Specials were disbanded to be replaced by the Ulster Defence Regiment. The UDR was meant to be a mixed force but by November 1972 it was 96% Protestant.

2. The government did not change the Special Powers Act.

3. Election rules were changed to treat all people equally.

4. The government agreed to new, fair boundaries. They were not ready until May 1973.

5. One Catholic was brought into the Cabinet in October 1971.

6. A fair 'points system' was introduced for giving out council houses.

Solution 2: Internment

The last Stormont Prime Minister was Brian Faulkner. He came to power in March 1971, at a time when the Provos were mounting a massive bombing campaign. There were 304 explosions in Northern Ireland between January and July 1971. Faulkner made a fateful decision to stop the violence: he decided to bring in internment. This was meant to be used against all suspected terrorists – Protestants as well as Catholics.

Why did Faulkner introduce internment? As a young politician, he had helped to deal with the last outbreak of IRA violence in 1956–62. Internment had been used then and it had worked. Faulkner tried to learn a lesson from history.

Faulkner's hope that 'history would repeat itself' proved disastrously wrong. In the months after internment the Provisional IRA went from strength to strength. Internment cause massive resentment among the Catholic community. Many of the people arrested were not involved in the IRA, and this increased further Catholic anger. The result was completely counter-productive – far from destroying the IRA, internment strengthened the IRA. The violence of some Catholics increased the fears of working-class Protestants. Loyalist vigilante groups gained new recruits: in September 1971 the Ulster Defence Association (UDA) was formed. The Unionist politicians were losing control over both the Catholic and the Protestant communities.

SOURCE 1

By mid-December 1971, 1,576 people had been arrested by the army under the Special Powers Act – virtually all of them Catholic. That meant almost 1,576 families who had experienced the shock of arrest often in the early hours of the morning and without much tenderness.

From a report by the *Sunday Times* 'Insight Team', 1972.

SOURCE 2

Anti-internment protest in London.

SOURCE 3

Hooding – detainees were kept fully hooded except when interrogated or in rooms by themselves

Noise – when detainees were held together they were subjected to a continuous hissing noise

Sleep – it was the general policy to deprive men of sleep during the early days of the operation

Extract from the 'The Compton Report' an official British Government report, 1971

Solution 3: The British Army

When British troops went into Northern Ireland there was rejoicing among many Catholics. They were not keen to see the return of the IRA and thought that the soldiers would protect them from Protestant violence. Catholics gave tea and sandwiches to the newly arrived British forces. This friendly atmosphere did not last long.

SOURCE 4

British soldiers being attacked by Catholic youths, 1972.

❖ *Look at the following sources. Why did the good relationship between the British Army and the Catholic community break down?*

SOURCE 5

It was not long before occasional clumsy brutality on the part of the British forces provoked an angry reaction from the population. It was not difficult for an IRA, trying to control Catholic areas of Derry and Belfast, to use this reaction for their own ends.

Robert Kee, *Ireland – A History*, 1980.

SOURCE 6

The Army was designed and trained to be aggressive. . . On 27th June, 1970, for the first time, armed Provisionals appeared on the streets to challenge the UVF. The gun battle which followed lasted all night. There were five dead, four of them Protestants. The army's response was to get tough. On 3rd July a search for arms in Catholic areas led to allegations of damage to property by the soldiers. All the local people were forced by the Army to stay in their houses, this curfew lasted 36 hours. Four people were killed and the army's conduct ensured the hostility of the Catholic Ghettoes.

Taylor Downing, *The Troubles*, 1980.

SOURCE 7

A Belfast docker, John Benson, painted 'No Tea Here' on the wall of his street – a reference to the practice of giving tea to the troops. The army complained to the police. Deciding that the slogan was 'an obvious attempt to intimidate people', the magistrate gave Benson six months for breach of the peace.

The *Sunday Times* 'Insight Team', 1972.

SOURCE 8

Catholic graffiti.

◆ *Look back at pages 72 – 74. Explain in your own words how each of the three solutions failed to solve the crisis.*

◆ *Do you think it was inevitable that these attempted solutions would fail?*

Bloody Sunday – the last straw

The failure of the British army to end the crisis became clear to the whole world on 30 January 1972. Thirteen unarmed men were shot dead by members of the Parachute Regiment during a Civil Rights march in Derry.

Ever since people have argued about who fired the first shot. What no one disputes is that the deaths on Bloody Sunday led to a great outburst of Catholic anger and were the final nail in the coffin of the Stormont government. Bernadette Devlin was an eyewitness to the shootings and a member of the House of Commons. During a debate in the London

Parliament she called the British minister, Reginald Maudling, a 'murdering hypocrite' and slapped him across the face. In Dublin 20,000 people attacked the British Embassy and burned it down. The IRA stepped up its campaign with bombs in England and Northern Ireland.

The British actions were condemned throughout the world. The Prime Minister, Ted Heath, decided that firm action was necessary and he suspended the Stormont government on 24 March.

SOURCE 11

When the army started shooting that day the first reaction, after fear, was bewilderment. Why were they shooting? At Free Derry corner, where most people had gathered, the crowd flung themselves to the ground. Looking up one could see stragglers running panic-stricken, bounding over the barricade, three of them crumpling to the ground. An hour and a half later no one knew for certain how many were dead. Some said three, some five. (It was actually thirteen.)

Later an IRA man said 'Our military orders after "Bloody Sunday" were to kill every British soldier we could'.

Eamon McCann, *War in an Irish Town*, 1974.

SOURCE 10

Civil Rights marchers confront the army at barricades before the shootings on 30 January 1972.

SOURCE 9

Civil Rights marchers on Bloody Sunday

5: THE FAILURE OF POWER-SHARING

Since the fall of Stormont in 1972, British leaders have tried to find a new system of government for Ulster which would satisfy both Catholics and Protestants. The British believed that the Unionist-dominated Stormont government had failed and that Northern Ireland needed a government in which both sides shared power.

In June 1973 the British government arranged fair elections for a Northern Ireland Assembly. The Unionist Party won the majority of seats but some of their leaders got together with the largely Catholic SDLP and agreed together on a plan for power-sharing. This meant setting up a Northern Ireland Executive including Nationalists as well as Unionists. The Irish Republic took part in these talks and gave its backing to the Executive. It was also agreed to set up a Council of Ireland with representatives form the North and the South.

Why did the Power-Sharing experiment fail?

The Power-Sharing Executive took over on 1 January 1974 headed by the Unionist leader, Brian Faulkner, and SDLP leader Gerry Fitt. Even before they began work they were widely condemned by sections of the Protestant community.

◆ *Look at the following sources.*
◆ *Using these sources explain why many Protestants were so opposed to power-sharing?*

SOURCE 1

Ian Paisley. Paisley was one of the leading critics of power-sharing. Later he explained why he disliked the idea so much.

Catholics don't want a share in the government of Northern Ireland. They want Northern Ireland to be destroyed, and to have a united Ireland. Even if they were to join a government it's only until such time as they can destroy the government and the state.

SOURCE 2

The more militant Protestants reached the stage by the end of 1971 in which they identified the whole Catholic community with the IRA

An Irish historian, T. W. Moody, explained that even the moderate SDLP was greatly distrusted by some Protestants, 1974.

SOURCE 3

Working-class Protestants celebrate the end of power-sharing.

A general strike

In May 1974 a group of leading working-class Protestants, known as the Ulster Workers' Council, called a general strike. This aimed to bring the whole of Northern Ireland to a standstill and 'break' the Power-Sharing Executive.

The Ulster Workers' Council strike began on 14 May 1974. At first it was not taken seriously by very many people. On May 15 the Belfast correspondent of *The Times* wrote, 'It seems likely that Belfast will suffer no more than a slight loss of power during the day-time hours.' Two days later a British minister, Stan Orme, said, 'We're going to break this strike. I can tell you this – you're wasting your time. There is no question of negotiation with these bigots.' But the strike soon became very serious. UDA road blocks paralysed Belfast: petrol and electricity were severely limited.

By May 27 the strike had escalated even more. The strikers threatened a complete shut-down at the electricity power stations and sewage pumping stations. Faced with this awful prospect, Faulkner resigned on May 28 and the Power-Sharing Executive came to an end. For the first time in Irish or British history an administration had been brought down by a general strike.

SOURCE 5

A cartoon commenting on the role of the Protestant private armies in the strike.

SOURCE 6

The people on this side of the water – British parents – have seen their sons spat upon and murdered. British taxpayers have seen the taxes they have poured out, almost without regard to cost, going into Northern Ireland. They see property destroyed by evil violence and are asked to pick up the bill for rebuilding it. Yet people who benefit from this now viciously defy Westminster, people who spend their lives sponging on Westminster and British democracy. Who do these people think they are?

Harold Wilson, British Prime Minister, in a television message, 25 May 1974.

SOURCE 7

Wilson's speech deeply offended many Protestant people and increased support for the strike. A British journalist, Robert Fisk, later wrote this about the impact of the speech.

The UWC were delighted. Glen Barr, their leader, said later that they thought of making Wilson an 'honorary' member of the Ulster Workers' Council.

'Any hope he had of wrecking the strike went with that speech,' he said.

❖ *What did the Protestant strikers do to bring down the power-sharing Executive?*

❖ *How did the speech of Harold Wilson help the strikers?*

SOURCE 4

Strikers' blockade and march on Stormont, 1974.

6: THE HUNGER STRIKES, 1981

When the IRA re-appeared on the streets of Derry and Belfast in 1970 they said they had come to protect the Catholic community from Protestant violence. They got a mixed reception. Some Catholics did welcome them as protectors. Many merely tolerated the IRA because they were too afraid to do otherwise. Others, however, spoke out against violence of all kinds. By the end of 1970 a new peaceful Nationalist party had been formed – the SDLP. The SDLP was keen to find peaceful ways of sorting out differences with the Unionists. In 1976 two Catholics, Mairead Corrigan and Betty Williams, founded the Women's Peace Movement. Over the next two years they organised a series of peace marches which were supported by people on both sides. For a time there seemed a chance that the IRA would again be rejected by the Catholic community, as they had been during the 1956–62 bombing campaign.

Then, in 1981, a group of IRA prisoners in the Maze Prison (in cells known as H blocks) began a hunger strike. This hunger strike was the climax of several years of prison protest in Northern Ireland. Since the start of the recent conflict, Nationalist prisoners have insisted that they should not be treated like ordinary criminals. The British government agreed to their demands in 1972, and gave 'special category' privileges to prisoners who had committed crimes for political reasons. They included no longer having to wear prison uniform or to do prison work.

In 1976 the British changed this policy and abolished the 'special category'. The IRA prisoners in the Maze Prison reacted to the changed rules by starting the 'blanket protest'. They refused to wear prison clothes and remained naked, except for blankets. In 1978 the prisoners stepped up their pressure by soiling their cells with their own excrement. The British refused to grant a return to special category, and in 1980 the IRA and INLA decided on a hunger strike. The first hunger strike ended in confusion in December, but on 1 March Bobby Sands began his fast. The British Prime Minister Margaret Thatcher insisted on not giving in to Sands and the other hunger strikers. By October ten men were dead and the hunger strike was called off.

SOURCE 1

The hunger strike has a long tradition. The funeral of the Nationalist Terence McSwiney, mayor of Cork, who died after going on hunger strike in 1920.

SOURCE 2

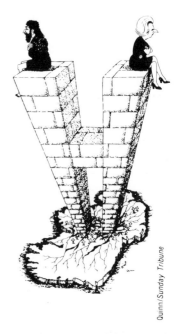

Quinn/*Sunday Tribune*

Cartoon: Thatcher and the H Block protest.

SOURCE 3

He knows that if he dies, through his death, there will be so much anger stored up in the Irish people that it will fuel the struggle for the next ten years.

Danny Morrison, Sinn Féin, speaking about Bobby Sands, March 1981.

SOURCE 4

There is no such thing as political murder, political bombing or political violence. We will not compromise on this. There will be no political status.

Margaret Thatcher's reaction, March 1981.

The consequences of the Hunger Strikes

The hunger strikers won much support among ordinary Catholics.

SOURCE 6

There were people on the marches against the government's treatment of the hunger strikers who had never been on a march before. Never was there such a determination among the mass of people to have done with the British government. It was now possible to speak respectfully of the IRA.

Des Wilson, a Catholic priest from Belfast, October 1981.

SOURCE 7

When Bobby Sands died many of us felt it's back to square one. If you tried to call a peace rally now you wouldn't get anyone to come. There is far more bitterness and a feeling of anti-Britishness.

Mairead Corrigan, leader of the Women's Peace Movement, December 1981.

SOURCE 8

We were led to believe that only a minority of Catholics supported violence. To Protestants the hunger strike showed that Catholics were prepared to support the gunmen who murdered their fellow citizens.

Protestants were dismayed at the widespread Catholic support for the Hunger Strike: Frank Millar, Official Unionist Party, May 1983.

SOURCE 9

Ten people had the courage to stand by their country to the point of dying for it. The H Block issue became a worldwide issue. The Republican movement gained enormously in the number of people who joined, in favourable publicity and in finance.

Daithi O'Conaill, Sinn Féin, December, 1981

The level of Catholic support for the hunger strikers and the IRA was shown to the whole world in May 1981 when between 50,000 and 100,000 people went to the funeral of Bobby Sands. The rise in support for Sinn Féin after the Hunger Strikes was to have dramatic consequences for the North of Ireland. The British government became concerned at the possibility of Sinn Féin replacing the moderate, non-violent SDLP, as the voice of the Catholics of Northern Ireland. The need to support the SDLP led, in turn, to the Anglo-Irish Agreement of 1985. For Sinn Féin/IRA, the Hunger Strikes showed that there were other ways of winning support for the republican cause in addition to the use of violence. The Hunger Strikes led Sinn Féin to become involved in ordinary politics.

❖ *What happened during the Hunger Strike crisis?*
❖ *Why do you think the IRA prisoners went on hunger strike?*
❖ *What were the results of the Hunger Strike?*

7: THE 1998 PEACE DEAL

After the Hunger Strike of 1981, Sinn Féin moved towards greater involvement in ordinary politics. At first Sinn Féin leaders spoke about using 'the ballot and the bullet' to take power. Some leaders, including Gerry Adams, were prepared to consider abandoning the bullet altogether. During the first half of the 1980s Sinn Féin and the SDLP had fought a bitter battle for Catholic votes. Eventually this struggle reached deadlock.

Throughout the 1980s the Catholic Church put pressure on the Sinn Féin leaders to look for a peaceful settlement. Individual Catholic priests (and also some Presbyterian ministers) acted as go-betweens and messengers. Alec Reid, a Catholic priest from Belfast, brought John Hume and Gerry Adams together for talks in the late 1980s and early 1990s.

SOURCE 3
John Hume, leader of the SDLP. In December 1998 he and David Trimble received the Nobel Peace Prize.

SOURCE 1

As everybody now knows, the patience, skill and determination shown by clergy has been nothing less than indispensable in bringing about the peace we now enjoy. I can say that without them the present hopeful situation would not and could not have come about.

John Hume, December 1995.

In 1983 a leading Catholic bishop, Dr Cahal Daly, challenged Sinn Féin to look at peaceful ways of making political progress. Gerry Adams replied in a way that made it clear that he was prepared to consider different approaches, but he needed to be convinced that they would work.

SOURCE 2

You call on Republicans to renounce violence and join in the peaceful struggle for the rights of Nationalists. What peaceful struggle? Those who condemn the armed struggle have a responsibility to spell out an alternative course by which Irish independence can be secured. I, for one, would be pleased to consider such an alternative.

Gerry Adams, 1983.

By the late 1980s the Sinn Féin leaders were convinced that new thinking was needed to break the stalemate. In 1988 Adams met John Hume to begin formal talks. The discussions were criticised by both the Unionists and the British government. Talks continued intermittently over the following years. Despite criticisms from other members of their two parties, the two men began to trust each other.

The British attitude

The British government also helped to create the atmosphere necessary for a cease-fire. They had decided early in the Troubles that the IRA could be contained, but not defeated, by the British army. British politicians knew that any settlement of the Northern Ireland problem was unlikely without all-party talks, including Sinn Féin.

In 1989 a new Northern Ireland Secretary, Peter Brooke, took office. He was keen to try new approaches to bring peace to Ireland. He tried to send messages to the IRA/Sinn Féin leaders, suggesting that there was scope for Sinn Féin to get involved in peace talks. He said publicly that the IRA would not be destroyed through the use of force. On 9 November 1990, Brooke made a speech announcing that Britain had 'no selfish strategic or economic interest in Northern Ireland'. He went on to say that Britain was ready to accept a united Ireland if that were the decision of the majority in Northern Ireland. In 1991 secret talks took place between Sinn Féin and senior civil servants.

Pressure from America

In the USA, a new President, Bill Clinton, came to power in 1993. He was keen to take an active role in Ireland. The US government was the most powerful in the world and had considerable influence over the government of the UK. Clinton's administration promised that there would be significant economic help for Ireland if a peaceful settlement could be achieved. Clinton signalled that he wanted to give Sinn Féin a chance by allowing Gerry Adams to visit the USA.

After the cease-fire of August 1994, Clinton tried to meet his side of the bargain. In 1995 he visited Belfast to express his support for peace.

SOURCE 4

I urge American businessmen and all others to consider investing in Northern Ireland and the Border counties. The workforce is well educated and well motivated. The productivity levels are high. The unit labour costs are low. The labour relations are good. The infrastructure, the communications, the access to the European market are fine.

Clinton encouraging American businesses to invest in Northern Ireland, 1995.

Continuing violence

The moves towards peace did not mean any reduction in the level of violence. The IRA staged a dramatic demonstration on 7 February 1991, when they attacked Downing Street with mortar bombs while the Cabinet was meeting. Public opinion in both Britain and Ireland was shocked in March 1993 by the explosion of a bomb in Warrington, in the north-west of England, killing two children. A month later a huge bomb in the financial district of London caused a massive £1 billion worth of damage to houses and offices.

In 1991–93 there was also a great increase in the number of killings carried out by Loyalist paramilitaries. Loyalist killings were soon greater in number than IRA killings. There was an increasing war-weariness among people in Northern Ireland. On 17 January 1992 eight Protestant workmen were killed by an IRA bomb. Their 'crime' was to carry out work for the security forces. A local journalist expressed a common sense that it was time for the politicians to become more active in looking for a settlement.

SOURCE 5

Eight died in Tyrone. The level of outrage rises so high. Still they refuse to come to the table. What if 50 died, or 150? What then? Do Paisley and Hume, the whole damn lot of them have a body count in their heads above which they will definitely begin to move heaven and earth to do something about it. Pick a number lads. Any number.

Emily O'Reilly, 1992.

After the Omagh bomb President Clinton and his wife visited the town with Tony and Cherie Blair.

The Hume-Adams Agreement was passed on to the Dublin government. The Irish Taioseach, Albert Reynolds, felt that the IRA would call a cease-fire if the British government made it clear that there would be talks about the future of Ireland. Reynolds contacted the British Prime Minister, John Major. They met and produced a document known as the Downing Street Declaration in December 1993.

SOURCE 6

The British government pledges to uphold the democratic wish of a greater number of the people of Northern Ireland on the issue of whether they prefer to support the union or a sovereign united Ireland. The British government have no selfish strategic or economic interest in Northern Ireland. Their primary interest is to see peace, stability and reconciliation established by agreement. They will work together with the Irish government to achieve such an agreement. The role of the British government will be to encourage, facilitate and enable the achievement of such an agreement through a process of dialogue and co-operation. The British government agree that it is for the people of Ireland alone, by agreement between the two parts, to exercise their right of self-determination on the basis of consent, freely and concurrently given, North and South, to bring about a united Ireland, if that is their wish.

The Irish government accepts the democratic right of self-determination by the people of Ireland as a whole must be achieved and exercised with and subject to the agreement and consent of a majority of the people of Northern Ireland and must respect the civil rights and liberties of both communities. . . In the event of an overall settlement, the Irish government will support a change in the Irish Constitution which would fully represent the principle of consent in Northern Ireland.

Extracts from the Downing Street Declaration.

Towards a cease-fire

Sinn Féin was uncertain how to respond. For months its leaders asked for 'clarification' of the Agreement. In March 1994 the IRA staged a mortar attack on Heathrow Airport to show that it still had the capacity to attack British targets. Adams was preoccupied with the need to avoid a split in the Republican movement, and so proceeded very slowly. After months of secret discussions the IRA finally agreed to stop the armed campaign on 31 August 1994.

Adams hoped that this cease-fire would quickly lead to negotiations about the future of Northern Ireland and rapid changes in the way Northern Ireland was organised.

SOURCE 7

Recognising the potential of the current situation and in order to enhance the democratic peace process and underline our commitment to its success, the leadership of the Irish Republican Army have decided that as of midnight, Wednesday 31 August, there will be complete cessation of military operations. All our units have been instructed accordingly.

IRA statement announcing a cease-fire, 31 August 1994.

After the cease-fire

The Sinn Féin leaders had taken a big risk in arguing for a cease-fire. There was a danger that the IRA would split into pro- and anti-cease-fire factions. Not all Republicans supported the idea of the cease-fire. Sinn Féin leaders hoped that the end of the violence would lead to rapid change in Northern Ireland and Sinn Féin involvement in talks about the future. This did not happen. British leaders were suspicious of the IRA: they wanted proof that the cease-fire was permanent. In 1995 the British government stated that the IRA must begin to hand over weapons before talks started. For the IRA leadership the 'de-commissioning' of weapons was a sign of surrender, and they were not prepared to hand over a single gun. Frustration on the part of the IRA grew, and in February 1996, seventeen months after the cease-fire, the IRA announced that the cease-fire was over. At the same time they exploded a bomb at Canary Wharf in London which killed two men.

As a result of the renewal of IRA violence the British government excluded Sinn Féin from any peace talks. Many felt a growing sense of anger while little was being achieved. In July, Loyalists showed their frustration by rioting and setting up road blocks all over Northern Ireland. The RUC had tried to stop an Orange Order march through a Catholic area at Drumcree, Portadown, but had been forced to back down after Protestants gathered in huge numbers. Meanwhile the IRA continued its mainland campaign. A huge bomb destroyed the central shopping area of Manchester in June 1996.

By early 1997 the peace process appeared to be going nowhere. The situation improved after a general election in the United Kingdom. In May 1997 Labour replaced the Conservatives as the party of government in Britain, and Tony Blair became Prime Minister. The new Labour government was very keen to get peace talks going in Northern Ireland. Mo Mowlam, the new Secretary of State for Northern Ireland, immediately made it clear that Sinn Féin could play a full part in the talks if the IRA renewed its cease-fire.

On 19 July 1997, the IRA announced the restoration of its cease-fire of 1994. Mo Mowlam welcomed this, and said that if the IRA cease-fire continued for six weeks then Sinn Féin could join negotiations. The cease-fire held, and on 29 August the Secretary of State announced that Sinn Féin was invited to talks. Negotiations involving the Irish and British governments and the parties of Northern Ireland began in October 1997. Many difficult months followed. Ian Paisley's DUP refused to take part. Extreme groups outside the talks almost wrecked everything. In December, INLA prisoners in the Maze Prison murdered the Loyalist Volunteer Force leader, Billy Wright. The LVF responded with sectarian killings of several Catholics. In early 1998 one of the small Loyalist parties and Sinn Féin were briefly expelled from the talks because they were linked to political killings. Despite these problems the negotiations continued, chaired by the American, Senator George Mitchell.

The British government did not want the talks to go on forever. They said that an agreement must be reached before 9 April 1998. The British and Irish governments, the SDLP and Sinn Féin all wanted to do a deal. They were ready to support a new power-sharing assembly in Northern Ireland. The Irish government was prepared to drop its longstanding claim to the whole of Ireland. What was not clear was whether the Ulster Unionist Party would agree. Without the support of this, the largest Unionist party, any agreement was doomed. As the deadline approached there was great pressure on David Trimble, leader of the Ulster Unionist Party. Many in his party were against a deal because it would lead to the rapid release of IRA prisoners. If he agreed to the deal he risked being seen as giving in to Nationalists. If he refused to do a deal, he might be labelled as the man who wrecked Northern Ireland's chance for peace.

Discussions continued late into the night on 9 April and, without a break for sleep, throughout the morning and afternoon of the following day, which was Good Friday. Trimble had reservations about the deal, but he finally decided that it was the best he could get, and he gave his agreement. The people of both Northern Ireland and the Republic of Ireland voted on the Good Friday Agreement in a referendum in May 1998. In Northern Ireland 71% said that they approved the deal: in the Republic 94% said 'yes'. A month later there were elections for the new assembly, which met for the first time on 1 July 1998. Trimble was chosen by the assembly as First Minister, with Seamus Mallon from the SDLP as his deputy.

The new assembly did not lead to any im[provements] improvements in the divided nature of N[orthern] Ireland. Many Unionists, including Ian Pais[ley's] DUP, opposed the work of the assembly. In 1998, as in previous years, there were bitter arguments throughout July about the routes of Orange marches, and particularly the Drumcree march. The 1998 marching season was overshadowed by the Loyalist killing of three young brothers, whose mother was Catholic. Arguments continued about the handing over of the weapons of the private armies. An extreme Republican group exploded a bomb in the town of Omagh in August 1998, killing 29 people. David Trimble of the Ulster Unionists and John Hume of the SDLP were awarded the Nobel Peace Prize for their work on the Agreement. However, there was much to be done before the Good Friday Agreement could be said to have led to peace in Ireland.

What were the causes of the peace agreement of 1998? In your answer you could mention:
- *the influence of the Catholic Church;*
- *the Hume-Adams talks;*
- *Loyalist killings;*
- *pressure from America;*
- *the Downing Street Declaration.*
- *the 1997 general election;*
- *David Trimble.*

SOURCE 8

A Catholic woman pleads with Orangemen not to march down the Nationalist Garvaghy Road, Drumcree, Portadown, in July 1996.

THE TURNING POINT THAT NEVER WAS: CHURCHILL OFFERS A UNITED IRELAND, 1940

In the autumn of 1939 Britain went to war with Germany. By May 1940 the war was going badly and Neville Chamberlain, the Prime Minister, resigned. He was replaced by Winston Churchill who eventually led Britain to victory. Churchill had long taken an interest in Irish politics, and in 1921 he had been involved in the Irish Treaty negotiations.

Sir Winston Churchill

SOURCE 1

Long before the Second World War, Churchill had made a commitment to the Protestants of Northern Ireland:
England will defend Ulster as if it were Kent or Lancashire. We could no more allow hostile hands to be laid upon the Protestant north than we could allow the Isle of Wight to fall into the hands of the Germans. Until Ulstermen wish to abandon the British Empire, the British Empire will never abandon them.

Winston Churchill, *The Daily Mail*, February 1933.

During its very first days Churchill's government made an offer to the Dublin government that broke the promise of 1933. The following document was made public in 1980, forty years after it was drawn up.

SOURCE 2

The 1940 offer of unification made to Eamon de Valera on 28 June 1940:

(i)   A declaration will be made by the UK government immediately accepting the offer of a United Ireland. The declaration will give a solemn promise that the Union is to become at an early date an accomplished fact from which there shall be no turning back.

(ii) British naval vessels will have the use of ports in Eire and other British forces will be stationed in Eire.

(iii) The Government of Eire will arrest all Germans and Italians in the country.

British government document of June 1940.

SOURCE 3

Modern historians summarise the problems facing Churchill in 1940:
The war began disastrously for Britain and her allies. German square helmets became a familiar sight in Western Europe. The German forces poured across Holland, Belgium, Denmark and Norway. By May 1940 the British army were stranded in the Channel port of Dunkirk, but, by an incredible feat, her shattered army was evacuated under the nose of the Germans. On June 22 1940, France surrendered. Britain now stood alone. There was nothing to stop Hitler invading Britain except a handful of RAF fighters, a defeated army and badly equipped Home Guards.

Adapted from P. Darvill and W. Stirling, *The Exploding Years*, 1974.

SOURCE 4

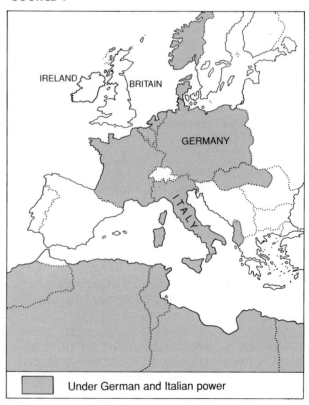

Under German and Italian power

German occupied Europe, June 1940.

How did the Northern Ireland government respond to the British offer of unification?

SOURCE 5

AM PROFOUNDLY SHOCKED AND DISGUSTED BY YOUR LETTER MAKING SUGGESTIONS SO FAR REACHING BEHIND MY BACK AND WITHOUT ANY PRE-CONSULTATION WITH ME. TO SUCH TREACHERY TO LOYAL ULSTER I WILL NEVER BE A PARTY.

The Northern Ireland Prime Minister reply to Churchill: telegram sent by Lord Craigavon to the British government, 27 June 1940.

How did the South respond?

SOURCE 6

We are unable to accept the plan. The plan would involve our entry into the war. Our people would be quite unprepared for it, and Dáil Éireann (the Dublin parliament) would certainly reject it.

We are, of course, aware that a policy of neutrality has its dangers. But, on the other hand, our entry into the war would involve us in dangers greater still. The plan gives no guarantee that in the end we would have united Ireland. Lord Craigavon could prevent unification by demanding concessions to which the majority of the Irish people could not agree.

Eamon de Valera to the British government, 4 July 1940.

SOURCE 7

He did undoubtedly believe that Craigavon would try to sabotage the plan for Irish unity. The British had gone back on their 1921 promise to negotiate the border in favour of the twenty-six counties. Could they be trusted to ensure Northern Ireland's co-operation in 1940, if necessary against the province's will? De Valera did not want a second generation of young Irishmen to die in another European war. It was scarcely ignoble of him to think that Britain was about to be defeated. If Britain had lost the war, Eire would inevitably have been occupied by German troops.

A historian's view of de Valera's decision. Robert Fisk, *In Time of War*, 1983.

SOURCE 8

A British newspaper cartoon on the refusal of Eire to join the fight against Germany.

❖ Look at Sources 1 and 2. In what way was there a change in Churchill's position on Ireland between 1933 and 1940?

❖ Look at Sources 3 and 4. Why did Churchill offer Irish unity in 1940?

❖ Why did de Valera reject the offer of Irish unity in 1940?

De Valera

Lord Craigavon (James Craig)

IRISH POLITICS AND BRITISH STRATEGY

In the years from 1500 to 1914, many European countries built up overseas empires. By 1914 they controlled large areas of the world. The most powerful of these world empires was the British Empire. Ireland was part of Britain's empire for around 400 years. In fact, Ireland was one of Britain's first colonies, conquered at about the same time as the West Indies and parts of America. Over the centuries Britain struggled with other European countries – Spain, France and Germany – to establish world supremacy. The government in London saw Ireland as a weak link in British defences: British leaders were concerned that their European enemies might use Ireland as a base for an attack on Britain itself. For this reason the British were determined to control Ireland. Ireland had a special strategic importance within the Empire because it was so close to Britain. At the closest point, only 20 kilometres separate Ireland and Great Britain. Ireland dominates the west coast of Britain. British fears were confirmed by the fact that Britain's enemies tried many times to land troops in Ireland as a first stop to conquering Britain.

SOURCE 1

'The plum pudding in danger'. An English cartoon of 1805 showing the world as a pudding being carved up by British and French leaders.

SOURCE 2

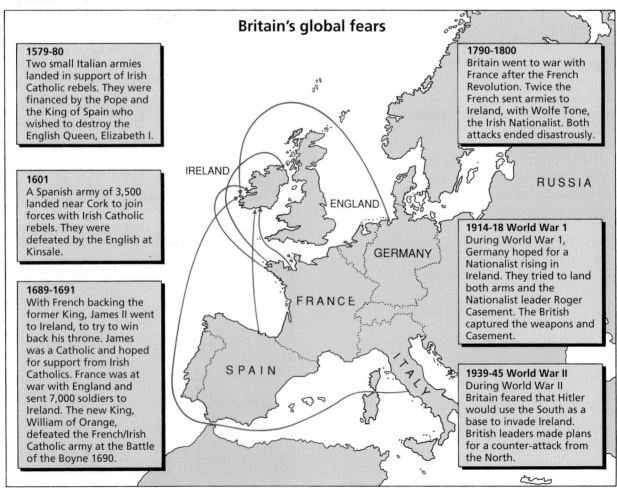

Britain's global fears

1579-80
Two small Italian armies landed in support of Irish Catholic rebels. They were financed by the Pope and the King of Spain who wished to destroy the English Queen, Elizabeth I.

1601
A Spanish army of 3,500 landed near Cork to join forces with Irish Catholic rebels. They were defeated by the English at Kinsale.

1689-1691
With French backing the former King, James II went to Ireland, to try to win back his throne. James was a Catholic and hoped for support from Irish Catholics. France was at war with England and sent 7,000 soldiers to Ireland. The new King, William of Orange, defeated the French/Irish Catholic army at the Battle of the Boyne 1690.

1790-1800
Britain went to war with France after the French Revolution. Twice the French sent armies to Ireland, with Wolfe Tone, the Irish Nationalist. Both attacks ended disastrously.

1914-18 World War 1
During World War 1, Germany hoped for a Nationalist rising in Ireland. They tried to land both arms and the Nationalist leader Roger Casement. The British captured the weapons and Casement.

1939-45 World War II
During World War II Britain feared that Hitler would use the South as a base to invade Ireland. British leaders made plans for a counter-attack from the North.

IRELAND
ENGLAND
RUSSIA
GERMANY
FRANCE
SPAIN
ITALY

Ireland and Britain's enemies.

'Ireland must be kept'

For over three hundred years Britain's enemies tried to use Ireland and Irish Catholics to destroy Britain. This affected Britain's attitude to Irish demands for independence in the 19th century.

SOURCE 3

Ireland must be kept, like India, at all costs: by persuasion if possible, if not by force.

Lord Salisbury, Conservative politician, 1872.

Britain and the South 1921–80

After British leaders finally gave independence to the Irish Free State in 1921, they remained worried about the threat to Britain's security. For this reason they kept control of three southern ports until 1937. When the Second World War broke out in 1939 the British feared that Hitler would invade Ireland as a first stage towards taking over Britain. Churchill, the British Prime Minister, tried to persuade Irish leaders to join the war on Britain's side by offering to reunite Ireland. De Valera refused this offer and insisted on staying out of the fighting.

After 1945 the Irish government refused to take sides in the 'Cold War' between Russia and other western countries, including Britain. The Republic tried to maintain a neutral position and refused to join NATO – the anti-Soviet military alliance. Some people believe that this made Britain more determined to hold onto Northern Ireland as a strategic base.

SOURCE 4

Throughout history Ireland, which has never been able to protect herself against invasion, it has always been a potential base of attack on the United Kingdom. It is important that a part of that island should wish to remain part of the United Kingdom and its defence system.

British Commonwealth Office, 1951.

SOURCE 5

The Tories are obsessed by the Russian threat to Europe. This has made Britain conclude that she needs a strategic armed force in Ireland to guard the Atlantic sea routes to Britain.

Daithi O'Connaill, Provisional Sinn Féin, 1982.

A changing approach to strategy

From the early 1980s the threat of the south of Ireland being used against Britain in a war became increasingly unlikely. Both the Republic and the UK had joined the European Union and there was no prospect of them being on different sides in a major war. In 1983 the Irish government told the British government that they would never allow their territory to be used as a base for attacks on Britain. The end of the Cold War in the late 1980s further helped the situation. In 1989 eastern Europe broke away from Soviet control. In 1991 the USSR disintegrated into many separate countries, of which the largest was Russia. The threat of war from the East evaporated and Britain could afford to take a more relaxed view of its military needs. Peter Brooke, the British Secretary of State for Northern Ireland, signalled the new view in 1990.

SOURCE 6

The British Government has no selfish strategic or economic interest in Northern Ireland.

Peter Brooke, November 1990.

❖ *What evidence is there in this unit that Britain has, in the past, wanted to control Ireland as part of its plans for the defence of Britain?*
❖ *What difference did the end of the Cold War make to Britain's defence plans?*

BRITISH RACISM AND THE IRISH

Until the 20th century the British looked on the Empire as vitally important for their future as a rich and powerful nation. Many British settlers went out to the colonies, like the Protestants of the Ulster Plantation. Some organised loyal governments, others ran the plantations, mines and trading companies which supplied Britain's food and raw materials. But most of these colonies also had native people who had lived there long before the British arrived. How important were they to their British masters?

◆ *Look at the following sources. What do they tell us about British attitudes towards the Irish?*
◆ *How far have attitudes towards the Irish changed over time?*

SOURCE 1

The Irish are wild, unfriendly people. They live like beasts. They grow little food in their fields. The soil is not to blame but the laziness of the people. Above all people, they cannot be trusted. When they give their word to anyone, they do not keep it. Their beards, clothes and minds are so barbarous that they cannot be said to have any culture.

Giraldus Cambrensis, *History and Topography of Ireland*, written in the 12th century.

SOURCE 2

I am haunted by the human chimpanzees I saw along that hundred miles of horrible country. I don't believe they are our fault. I believe there are not only more of them than of old, but that they are happier, better, more comfortably fed and lodged under our rule than they ever were. But to see white chimpanzees is dreadful; if they were black one would not feel it so much.

English novelist, Charles Kingsley, in a letter to his wife, July 1860.

SOURCE 3

Paddy: 'What happens if this bomb goes off in the car?'

Mick: 'It's alright – there's another one in the boot.'

A modern 'Irish joke'

SOURCE 4

A British view of the IRB as sub-humans, 1882. The IRB men had just murdered the British Chief Secretary to Ireland in Dublin.

SOURCE 5

A British view of the IRA as sub-humans, *The Spectator*, 1974.

SOURCE 6

The Birmingham Six on release from prison, 1991.

Attitudes towards the Irish and the system of justice

Anti-Irish feeling in Britain has always risen when there has been any IRA attack on mainland Britain. The mistrust of Irish people almost certainly led to a number of important miscarriages of justice during the recent conflict in Ireland. In turn, these miscarriages of justice have affected the way many Nationalists view Britain. In their eyes the British system of justice is biased against Irish people.

Four people were jailed in 1975 for the IRA bombing of a pub in Guildford, in southern England. The bombing had taken place in the previous year and five people had been killed. The prisoners became known as the 'Guildford Four'. A campaign was launched claiming that they had only confessed as a result of police brutality. Many years later, in 1989, the British courts agreed that the convictions were unsound and released three of the Four (the remaining prisoner was released later).

In 1974 the IRA bombed two pubs in the centre of Birmingham. No warnings were given and 19 people were killed. Two more people died later and many were badly injured. The British police arrested six Irishmen and charged them with the bombings. Almost certainly the men were beaten up by the police and by prison warders. They made confessions but they said later that these had been beaten out of them and were false. Although found guilty and sentenced to life imprisonment the 'Birmingham Six' continued to protest their innocence. After sixteen years in jail the Birmingham Six were finally released in 1991 on the orders of the British Court of Appeal. The Court accepted the men's claims that police had forged documents and lied in order to get them convicted.

Also in 1991, seven members of the Maguire family were finally cleared by the Court of Appeal of terrorist offences. They had served sentences ranging in length from four years to fourteen years. One of the family had died while in jail. They had originally been found guilty in 1976 of handling explosives intended for IRA bombs.

Despite the evidence from these cases that British police officers had deliberately lied in court, no policemen were ever convicted of any offences relating to the miscarriages of justice.

❖ *What happened to the Guildford Four and the Birmingham Six?*
❖ *Why do you think these stories have made many people unhappy about aspects of justice in Britain?*

THE IMPACT OF THE AMERICAN AND FRENCH REVOLUTIONS

The 18th century was a period of great change in ideas. People in America and France set up new kinds of government. These political changes had a powerful impact on Ireland, and the influence of the revolutions of the 18th century continues to the present day. In 1776 the Americans declared themselves to be independent of Britain. In 1789 French people took power from the king and his nobles and began the French Revolution. In both countries the new governments were 'republican'; they rejected the idea that they should be ruled by kings.

People in Ireland were interested in developments in America and France. News of faraway revolutions encouraged some Irishmen to develop Nationalist ideas. The first Irish Nationalists were Protestants. They were impressed by the way Americans had taken power from the British. Like the Americans, many wealthy Irish Protestants distrusted the way British managed their economy and wanted greater local control. In 1779 Protestants set up a military force known as the Irish Volunteers. At the time there was an Irish Parliament in Dublin, which was completely dominated by Protestants. Led by a man called Henry Grattan, the Irish Parliament declared in 1782 that it could make laws of its own and did not need the approval of the British Parliament in London.

French revolutionaries were more radical than their American counterparts. They called for 'Liberty, Equality and Fraternity'. The idea that all people might be treated equally was not widely held among powerful people at the time. These radical new notions of equality were welcomed by many Protestants in Ulster. Many northern Presbyterians welcomed the French Revolution. The newspaper, the Belfast News Letter, announced that the French Revolution was 'the greatest event in human history'. Some Protestants decided to imitate the French and they founded a group called the United Irishmen in 1791. The United Irishmen got much of their early support in Belfast, but their leader was a Dublin lawyer called Wolfe Tone. The United Irishmen said that all Irish people – whether Catholic or Protestant – should unite together to work for an independent Ireland.

SOURCE 1

Wolfe Tone and the leaders of the United Irishmen, 1798.

The British government was extremely frightened of French revolutionary ideas. Ministers feared that people in Britain and Ireland might copy the methods of the French and overthrow them. In 1794 they banned the United Irishmen. The organisation went underground and became more extreme in its views. When it was set up the United Irishmen had called for peaceful change. Later it became dedicated to a violent revolution. Tone fled to France and organised an armed force to invade Ireland. In 1796 Tone returned to Ireland with a fleet of 43 French ships and 15,000 French troops. Only bad weather stopped them from landing. In May 1798 the United Irishmen tried to stage a rebellion in Ireland. In most of Ireland the British forces had little difficulty in suppressing the rebellion. Tone attempted once again to invade with a French revolutionary force. He was captured on a French ship and committed suicide in prison.

Although the United Irishmen failed, their action had important consequences for the future of Ireland:

• In 1800 the Dublin Parliament was abolished, and Ireland came under the direct control of the London government. The British were determined to strengthen control over Ireland so that there could be no repetition of 1798. The new arrangements were set out in the Act of Union of 1800. Ever since, Irish people have been divided between Nationalists who want to end the power of the London parliament and Unionists who want to retain the spirit of the Act of Union.

• Wolfe Tone and the United Irishmen became heroes to some Nationalists. Ever since, revolutionary Nationalists have seen themselves as seeking to complete the work of Tone. His grave at Bodenstown in County Kildare is a place of pilgrimage for modern supporters of Sinn Féin/IRA, as well as some other Nationalists.

SOURCE 2

The grave of Wolfe Tone.

❖ *What impact did the American and French Revolutions have on Ireland?*
❖ *How successful was Wolfe Tone? Why do you think modern Republicans look back to Wolfe Tone as a hero?*
❖ *How did the rebellion of the United Irishmen lead to the Act of Union?*

Twentieth-century revolutionary movements

Irish Nationalists see themselves as the victims of imperialism. In the 20th century Nationalism has developed across the world, and in most colonies nationalists have forced the imperial power to leave. As in Ireland, nationalists in other countries have used a combination of peaceful and violent methods to win independence. Between 1945 and 1965 the British pulled out of country after country . This trend encouraged Irish Nationalists to think that one day the British would leave Ireland.

After 1968 there was a great rise in support for revolutionary groups across the world. Some of these groups have links with the IRA. For example, ETA wants the Basque people to break away from Spain and form a separate country. Like the IRA, ETA has consistently used bombing and murder the Spanish government.

Many revolutionary groups were encouraged by Colonel Gaddafi of Libya. Gaddafi is known to have supplied massive amounts of weaponry for the IRA. Libyan supplies included large amounts of a deadly plastic explosive known as Semtex.

Sinn Féin and the IRA have often seen parallels between their own struggle and that of the African National Congress (ANC) in South Africa, and the Palestinian Liberation Organisation (PLO) in the Middle East. Throughout the 1970s the ANC and the PLO used violence against the governments of South Africa and Israel respectively. In the 1980s both organisations moved away from the use of force and towards more peaceful political methods. The abandonment of force seemed to bear fruit for the ANC and the PLO: in 1993 the Palestinians signed a peace treaty with Israel giving the PLO control over some largely Palestinian areas, in 1994 the ANC took power in South Africa. The success of peaceful strategies by the PLO and the ANC encouraged Sinn Féin/IRA to agree to the cease-fire of 1994.

❖ *Who are the ANC and the PLO? Why do you think IRA/Sinn Féin members liked to compare themselves to the ANC and the PLO?*
❖ *Both the ANC and the PLO renounced violence in the 1990s. What impact did this have on IRA/Sinn Féin?*

THE IRISH-AMERICAN CONNECTION

Poverty and the threat of starvation drove millions of Irish people to emigrate during the 19th century. The heaviest period of emigration came during and immediately after the Great Famine of 1845–49. The population of Ireland fell dramatically from 8 million in 1841 to 4 million in 1901.

The emigrants went to many places across the world carrying with them strong anti-British feelings. The most popular destination was the USA; by 1870 there were nearly 2 million Irish-born people living in America. Ever since the famine and the emigration, some Irish-Americans have consistently supported the idea of driving the British out of Ireland by force.

The Fenians and Clan-na-Gael

The Irish Republican Brotherhood – IRB (The Fenians) was founded in America in 1858. It was dedicated to a violent overthrow of British rule in Ireland. Hundreds of Irish-Americans returned home, to take part in the disastrous Fenian Rising of 1867. Despite this failure, the Fenians remained strong in America. In the 1870s, a Fenian, John Devoy, set up a new Irish-American organisation. This was called Clan-na-Gael and it raised money in the USA for Irish Nationalists. In 1880 Clan-na-Gael organised a trip to America for Parnell, during which he collected £200,000.

Irish-Americans and the Easter Rising 1916

Both the IRB and Clan-na-Gael took part in the planning of the Easter Rising. One member, Tom Clarke, returned from New York in 1907 specifically to help organise a rebellion.

SOURCE 1

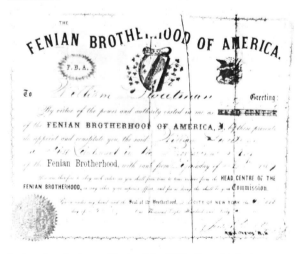

An American Fenian certificate of the 1860s. Since the famine violent Nationalism has always had Irish-American supporters.

SOURCE 2

There is not an Irishman in America today who would not rejoice to hear that a German Army was marching in triumph across England from Yarmouth to Milford Haven.

Even before 1916 anti-British feelings were common among Irish-Americans even before 1916: *The Chicago Citizen*, July 1908.

SOURCE 3

Feelings here about the executions and England was far more violent even than in Ireland. It became clear to me before I was 24 hours in New York that the Irish here had learned nothing and forgotten nothing since 1846.

T. P. O'Connor, a Parliamentary Nationalist, visited America in July 1917 and was surprised by the strength of feeling.

Noraid

Some Irish-Americans have continued to send help to the IRA, from its formation after the Easter Rising, right up to the present day. Support for the Provisional IRA has been organised since 1969 by a group knows as Noraid. It is estimated that Noraid raised £4 million for the Provisionals between 1970 and 1982. Members of Noraid have admitted smuggling arms to Northern Ireland.

SOURCE 4

Noraid fund-raising rally.

SOURCE 5

I've had enough of Irish-Americans, who haven't been back to their country for twenty or thirty years, come up to me and talk about the resistance, the revolution and the glory of the revolution. Where's the glory in bombing a Remembrance Day parade of old-age pensioners, the medals taken out and polished for the day? Where's the glory in leaving them dying under the rubble of a revolution that the majority of people in my country don't want.

American politicians and Ireland

John Hume of the SDLP has been responsible for getting the support of American politicians, including some who are not Irish-American. He hoped that the American government would put pressure on Britain to make changes in Northern Ireland. In the 1970s President Carter seemed willing to get involved in negotiating an Irish settlement. However, Presidents Reagan and Bush (1981–92) made it clear that they wanted nothing to do with the argument over Irish unity. Both valued the support of the British government in many areas of foreign policy and did not want to upset the British by getting involved in Irish politics.

SOURCE 6

St Patrick's Day parade in New York.

In November 1992 a new president was elected, Bill Clinton. He was determined to take a more active line on Ireland and in his election campaign he promised Irish-Americans that he would try to help in looking for a solution to the crisis in Northern Ireland. Pressure from Clinton on the governments in Dublin and London was one factor that helped in the signing of the Downing Street Declaration in 1993, which led to the cease-fire of 1994.

The USA played a central part in the negotiation of the 1998 peace deal. Clinton visited Northern Ireland in 1995 to show his support for the peace process. He was greeted with great enthusiasm by people from both communities. The chairman of the peace talks was American: George Mitchell, former US Senator and a friend of President Clinton. Clinton followed events with interest in the following years and took part, by phone, in the discussion that led to the Good Friday Agreement, 10 April 1998. To show his support, he visited Ireland in September 1998.

❖ *Why do many Irish-Americans have strongly anti-British views?*
❖ *What part did Irish-Americans play in the Fenian movement?*
❖ *What is NORAID?*
❖ *What part have American politicians played in recent Irish politics?*

ACKNOWLEDGEMENTS

Every effort has been made to contact the holders of copyright material but if any have inadvertently been overlooked, the publishers will be pleased to make the necessary arrangements at the first opportunity.

The publishers should like to thank the following for permission to reproduce photographs on these pages

T = top, B = bottom, R = right, C = centre, L = left

Associated Press Ltd 70;
Belfast Telegraph 5, 41, 52R, 69B;
C. Doyle/Camera Press, London 71;
J. Gray/Camera Press, London 89;
Century Newspapers 69T;
Corbis-Bettman/UPI 92/93;
Crawford Art Gallery, Cork 24;
Mary Evans Picture Library 10R, 15L, 17C, 18, 65, 86;
Fotomas Index 13, 43, 45;
Guardian 33, 36, 40;
Hulton Getty Picture Collection Ltd 9, 16, 19, 26, 27T, 56L, 64, 67T, 77B, 84, 85C&B;
The Trustees of the Imperial War Museum, London 23, 66CR;
The Irish Architectural Archive 14;
G. Peress/Magnum Photos 6L, 34T, 57, 75;
C. Steele-Perkins/Magnum Photos 38B;
Mansell Collection, London 17B, 46BL, 90;
Mirror Syndication 32BL;
National Library of Ireland 15R, 22, 27B, 44, 54, 55, 63, 66CL, 78T, 88T;
National Museum of Ireland 60BR, 62C;

Pacemaker Press 6R, 34B, 35T, 38CR, 40CR, 51L, 53, 58, 74R, 80;
PA News Picture Library 7, 81;
Popperfoto 32CL, 39T, 56R, 66TL, 73;
Popperfoto/Reuters 3, 20, 35C, 40B, 46CR, 83, 93T;
Slide File 47;
Spectator 88B;
Quinn/*Sunday Tribune* 78C;
Topham Picturepoint 39C, 60TL;
The Board of Trinity College, Dublin 10L, 11;
Ulster Folk and Transport Museum 51R;
By kind permission of the Trustees of the Ulster Museum 21, 52B, 59, 61, 67B;
Weidenfeld and Nicolson Archives 8, 12;
Writers and Readers Publishing Cooperative 77T.

Cover photograph: Pacemaker Press

The author and publishers gratefully acknowledge the following publications from which written sources in this book are drawn:

Robert Harbinson for an extract from R. Harbinson, *No Surrender – An Ulster Childhood*, Faber & Faber, 1960; Andre Deutsch Ltd for extracts from *The Price of My Soul* by Bernadette Devlin; *The Guardian*; David McKitterick, *The Independent;* Methuen & Co. Ltd for an extract from *Britain Between the Wars* by C. L. Mowat; Pluto Press for extracts from *War and an Irish Town* by Eamonn McCann; Schofield & Sims Ltd for an extract from *The Exploding Years* by P. A. Darvill and W. R. Stirling.

Published by Collins Educational,
An imprint of HarperCollins*Publishers*
77–85 Fulham Palace Road
London W6 8JB

www.**Collins**Education.com
On-line support for schools and colleges

© HarperCollins*Publishers* 1999

First published by Holmes McDougall Ltd, Edinburgh, 1987
This edition first published 1999

ISBN 0 00 327015 7

Reprinted 2001

General editor of the original edition:
Aileen Plummer

Tony McAleavy asserts the moral right to be identified as the author of this work.

British Library Cataloguing in Publication Data
A catalogue record for this book is available from the British Library.

Edited by Lorimer Poultney and Joanne Stone
Design by Sally Boothroyd
Cover design by Derek Lee
Illustrations by Raymond Turvey
Picture research by Caroline Thompson
Production by Anna Pauletti
Printed and bound in Hong Kong